Enter the exotic realm of

THE ILLUSTRATED

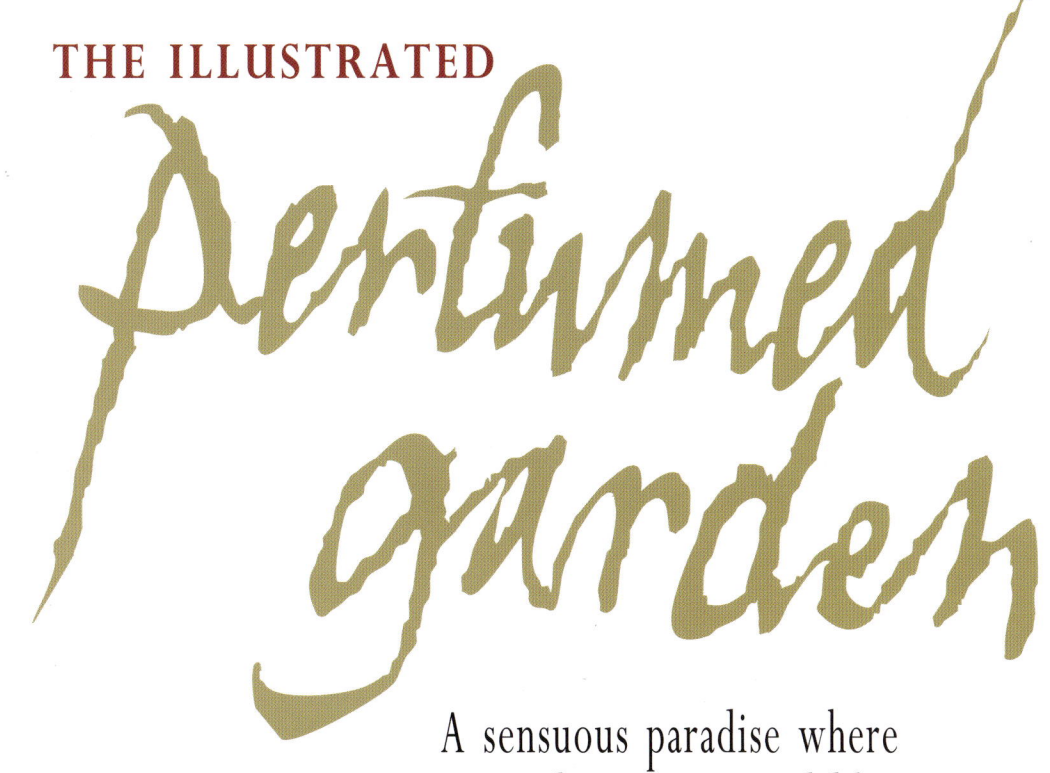

Perfumed garden

A sensuous paradise where
erotic love grows and blooms

Adapted by Jan Hutchinson,
Kirsty McKenzie and Ken Brass
Original text by Sheik Nefzawi
Original translation by Sir Richard Burton

HarperCollins*Publishers*

HarperCollins*Publishers*

First published in Australia in 1996
by HarperCollins*Publishers* Pty Limited
ACN 009 913 517
A member of the HarperCollins*Publishers* (Australia) Pty Limited Group

HarperCollinsPublishers
25 Ryde Road, Pymble, Sydney NSW 2073, Australia
1160 Battery Street, San Francisco, California 94111–1213, USA
Hazelton Lanes, 55 Avenue Road, Suite 2900, Toronto, Ontario M5R 3L2
and 1995 Markham Road, Scarborough, Ontario M1B 5M8 Canada
31 View Road, Glenfield, Auckland 10, New Zealand
77–85 Fulham Palace Road, London W6 8JB, United Kingdom
10 East 53rd Street, New York NY 10032, USA

National Library of Australia Cataloguing-in-Publication data:

Nafzãwĩ, 'Umar ib<u>n</u> Muhammad
[Rawd al-'ã,tir fĩ nuzhat ál-Khãtir. English]
Enter the exotic realm of the illustrated perfumed garden:
a sensuous paradise where erotic love grows and blooms

Includes index.
ISBN 0 7322 5697 6
1. Sex instruction - Early works to 1800. I. Burton,
Richard Francis, Sir, 1821-1890. II. Title. III. Title:
Rawd al-'ã,tir fĩ nuzhat ál-Khãtir. English.

613.96

Photography by Louise Lister
Illustrations by Selina Fitzgerald
Printed in Australia by Southbank Book

9 8 7 6 5 4 3 2 1
00 99 98 97 96

ACKNOWLEDGMENTS

Text and concept adapted from *The Perfumed Garden of the Shaykh Nefzawi:*
A Comprehensive Treatise on Love, translated by Sir Richard Burton, edited,
with an Introduction and Additional Notes by Alan Hull Walton,
HarperCollins*Publishers*, 1993.
'Introduction', 'Love-making Positions of *The Perfumed Garden*',
'Sex for all Shapes and Sizes', and quotes from the Sheik written
and adapted by Jan Hutchinson.
'Foreplay with an Eastern Edge', 'Scents for Sensuality and the Flavors of Passion',
'Bed, Bath, Table or Tent', 'Afterplay in the Eastern Way', 'Sex and Pregnancy',
'Safe Sex' and 'Loveplay' written by Kirsty McKenzie and Ken Brass.
Photography: Louise Lister.
Photography Assistant: Ben Harris.
Models: Kyla Natho and Matt Wise.
Hair and Make-up: Carmel Watkins and Leigh Evans.
Illustrations: Selina Fitzgerald.

CONTENTS

INTRODUCTION

*T*he *Perfumed Garden* is a classic work on the art of love-making written by Sheik Umar ibn Muhammed al-Nefzawi in Arabia during the 16th century. It was described by Alan Hull Walton, the editor of an early English-language edition, as 'a panegyric of love, a song of sensual delights, a collection of joyous imaginings, a work of rare and curious erotic knowledge'. And as a treatise on sexual pleasure, it rivals the equally fascinating *Kama Sutra*.

The contents of the original *Perfumed Garden* are far more extensive than might be expected from a simple sex manual — the Sheik's text covers a range of related subject matter, from the mechanics of love-play and intercourse to differences in human nature. And, as is evident from the Sheik's writings, in his eyes sex was not only a natural and enjoyable activity but one that was part of the divine design.

His work was, however, originally intended for men's eyes only. Ultimately, the Sheik saw the pleasures of love as a man's responsibility. Such an attitude is clearly at odds with that of many modern lovers but, on the whole, *The Perfumed Garden* is a work of considerable eroticism and scope, and today the essence of the Sheik's teachings applies as much to women as to men. As such, a brief outline of how this work came to the modern reader may throw some light on its ongoing significance.

A wide range of Arabian ideas began to infiltrate Western Europe long before the manuscript of *The Perfumed Garden* was discovered. The war lords of the Crusades in Europe had already brought back with them more than just the material spoils of their fighting — they had also discovered that there was much more to an active sexual life than their own cultures might have led them to believe! They had encountered, for instance, the idea that sexual love was an art, and that underpinning this art was a detailed wealth of physiological and anatomical knowledge.

They also came across new attitudes to sexual conduct, as well as some of the refinements of love-making, the likes of which today we may take for granted — personal hygiene, the delights of delayed orgasm, the significance of prolonged foreplay and the joys arising from mutually satisfying techniques of sexual stimulation, for instance.

All this knowledge was not, so far as we know, captured between two covers until a French officer stationed in Algeria in the middle of last century came across a manuscript version of the Sheik's text. Understandably, he was fascinated by its contents and set about translating it into his native language, completing the work by about 1850, but it was another quarter century or so before it was published. When it did finally appear, it was a lithograph edition of only 35 copies, each consisting of 283 pages of text and 43 erotic illustrations.

By 1885 this lithograph edition had been counterfeited in Paris. The following year *The Perfumed Garden* was set in type for the first time and a superb edition, limited to 220 copies, appeared. It is this version which caught the attention of Sir Richard Burton, and it is his direct translation of it from French into English on which this illustrated adaptation is based.

It should be clear, then, that *The Perfumed Garden* was quite a rare book. Certainly it was not one which most of the population would have had access to. And the history of how it came to be a more widespread treatise on the subject of sexual pleasure cannot fully be understood without explaining the origins of its publisher — the Kama Shastra Society.

The sole aim of the Kama Shastra Society was the translation and publication of rare and significant works of ancient origin that were concerned with love and sex. Its membership was ever only two: Sir Richard Burton himself, and his long-standing friend Forster Fitzgerald Arbuthnot; there was also an invisible patron, the distinguished Lord Houghton, who had a taste for erotic literature.

In all, five titles were published by the Society, including *The Perfumed Garden* in 1886, by which time the Society had already issued translations of the *Kama Sutra* and *Ananga Ranga*. In that same year, two editions of *The Perfumed Garden* were to appear, each bearing the sub-title 'A Manual of Arabian Erotology' and being for 'private circulation only'.

Through various publishing ploys, both editions maintained Burton's anonymity, but by 1888 an unexpurgated edition of his famed *Arabian Nights* was in wide circulation and so he embarked on a new version of *The Perfumed Garden*, this time translating directly from the Arabic and with much less concern than previously for secrecy. The new edition was to contain an extra, quite considerable chapter which had been left out by the French officer in his original translation.

This omitted chapter dealt with homosexuality. However, before he could complete translating it, Burton died. His wife, having never fully approved of her husband's publishing exploits, immediately burnt the entire manuscript, to the exasperation of scholars of the erotic ever since. Nevertheless, even Burton himself was aware of the importance that the book held, although he may not have had any inkling of the continued impact it would have for generations of lovers to come. 'I have put my whole life and all my life-blood into [it],' he said. 'It is my great hope that I shall live by it. It is the crown of my life.'

To date there have been many editions and thousands of copies of Burton's original translation published. The edition on which this book is

based was first compiled in 1963, with an extensive introduction and additional notes by Alan Hull Walton.

The Sheik's work, and its reverent style, are similar to those of other ancient love-making tracts. *The Perfumed Garden*'s discussion, though, is not limited to a list of explicitly described love-making positions. Included in the text are details of human sexual anatomy and physiology as well as of Eastern erotic techniques. It deals at length with the aphrodisiac qualities of certain foods, and outlines different perceived types of men and women according to body type and temperament. It includes a fascinating chapter on the sexual parts, enough to make any reader wonder how the Sheik conducted his research! Throughout, however, the mood is guilt-free — never is it contemplated that sex might be a questionable, let alone shameful, activity.

The Sheik also gives much practical advice, from details on how to avoid illnesses which may arise from sexual intercourse to warnings on excess. Above all, though, like other ancient treatises on the subject, *The Perfumed Garden* is designed to help both women and men avoid the sorts of monotony and boredom that might otherwise creep into a long-term sexual relationship, such as marriage. Its author is clearly concerned that partners realise that they may enjoy many years of love-making together, in a variety of manners, thereby lending to their union something of the excitement and affection that were there in the beginning.

Nevertheless, the Sheik's original text should perhaps be read in the light of his ancient Arabian cultural beliefs and practices. Modern readers may balk at some of his language, indeed at some of his turns of phrase. Contemporary writers of books on sex might be as loathe to use some of his expressions as contemporary lovers would! Even so, it should not be forgotten that Sheik Nefzawi's explicit explanations and descriptions were never intended to be coarse. Rather, they were meant to educate.

The Sheik valued the sanctity of a loving relationship and did not intend his text to be read as an open invitation to promiscuity or sexual license. Within the bounds of a loving relationship, a sound knowledge of sexual techniques, he believed, could only enhance the mutual affection.

This illustrated version of *The Perfumed Garden* has, then, been adapted and updated in keeping with the Sheik's own attitudes, with the addition of some new material. The chapter on foreplay reflects the utmost significance that the Sheik himself placed on it. Indeed, his writings contain much that is relevant to today's lovers — including the benefits of the judicious use of intoxicating scents to enhance their sexuality. The chapter on this aspect of love-making will inspire you to blend your own scents to produce the aromas conducive to arousal.

While many of us probably associate love-making with the bedroom, a wealth of locations awaits the imaginative couple. While the home itself offers several possibilities, there are other options — some carrying with them varying degrees of risk! The chapter 'Bed, Bath, Table or Tent' makes some creative suggestions.

The section on love-making positions describes numerous options. It draws directly on Sheik Nefzawi's own chapter 'Concerning Everything that is Favourable to the Act of Coition', although the language of his step-by-step instructions has been updated and simplified, and some brief commentary added, in the light of more recent sexual knowledge. 'Sex for all Shapes and Sizes' includes some additional variations for those partners whose bodily types might be a touch at odds with each other.

Pregnancy is, naturally, just one possible outcome of sex. But for some people it spells either the end of love-making or the temporary putting of it on hold. Neither need be the case, however, as is also explained and illustrated in that chapter.

'Afterplay in the Eastern Way' once again draws on the Sheik's own beliefs and practices. To put it simply, he recognizes the value of prolonging the feelings of intimacy after orgasm has been reached. The period we now know as 'afterplay' is, he insists, as much as part of having sex as anything else.

Some methods of enhancing sexual feelings have been around since ancient times, so the idea of helping things along on occasion is by no means a new one. If your imagination or desire leads you to exploring further the possibilities for love-making, then various inventive toys, tools and techniques are available to incorporate into your love-making. The chapter on 'Loveplay' looks at a range of these.

It would be negligent in this day and age not to include up-to-date information on 'safe sex'. Although some sexual health matters are discussed in *The Perfumed Garden*, the Sheik's advice does not include the problems contemporary lovers may face. An active sex-life has always carried some risks, but it was not until the advent of HIV and AIDS that sexually active people across the world met with the concept of 'safe sex'. But while lovers are actively making individual choices as to how to minimize the risks, such changes do not have to mean any diminishment in the sensational pleasures that are still to be had from sex.

Included as well throughout this book are enlightening quotes from the Sheik. Some of these are quaintly curious, though more often they show the extent of his profound sexual knowledge. His observations and advice — though not always in keeping with sexual attitudes of our times — still make for entertaining reading.

This book is for new lovers and long-time ones alike and it is hoped that this adaptation offers some glimpses into the joyous abandonment that is tantamount to sexual pleasure and will provide ongoing inspiration as you either embark on or continue the journey of your love-making life.

FOREPLAY
WITH AN EASTERN EDGE

Before 'setting to work with your wife,' says Sheik Nefzawi in *The Perfumed Garden*, 'excite her with toying, so that the copulation will finish to your mutual satisfaction.' Foreplay, for the Sheik, was crucial to great sex, as undeniably it still is.

'Play with her,' he urges. 'You will excite her by kissing her cheeks, sucking her lips and nibbling at her breasts. You will lavish kisses on her navel and thighs, and titillate the lower parts. Bite at her arms, and neglect no part of her body; cling close to her bosom, and show her your love and submission.'

In other words, love-making is a comprehensive business that takes time. Don't come home from the office, drag her from whatever she is doing and expect to be transported instantly to the perfumed garden of delights. The time and care and attention you contribute tends to correspond with the enjoyment you receive from love-making, although there are times and places when the alternative skills of the 'quickie' are demanded (see 'Bed, Bath, Table or Tent').

Things have changed between the Sheik's time and ours, as they had changed between the 16th-century *Perfumed Garden* and the *Kama Sutra*, 1,500 years earlier. *The Perfumed Garden* would originally have been a treatise that was kept from women's eyes, a manual of practical advice that was the business of men only. In enlightened modern relationships, however, what goes for the man goes for the woman, who likewise is not advised to arrive home from the office and lustfully drag her partner from the dinner he might be preparing.

But is the gap between the Sheik and contemporary love practices in fact as great as it might seem? 'Play,' Nefzawi urges the lovers he instructs — as do internationally recognized therapists today who say sex is the most important kind of adult play, and a form of play that is too often ignored in the 20th century.

Sheik Nefzawi says, 'Kiss … suck … nibble … bite'. So what has changed? In so many ways his could be a modern treatise. In fact, what has changed has often been to the detriment of our sex lives. Too many other influences intrude: too many messages, too many competing, conflicting demands; too often we ignore the lessons spelt out so clearly in *The Perfumed Garden*.

Although India, the land of the origin of the *Kama Sutra*, can now be stultifyingly puritanical, it is sometimes surprising how much the India of Vatsyayana and the Arabia of Sheik Nefzawi have in common with modern sensual teachings in the West. Those who surf the Internet for turn-ons might argue otherwise, although the teachings of both Vatsyayana and Nefzawi are accessible on the Net. Electronic, automatic or manual, the importance of foreplay remains paramount. And thanks to the great teachers from the Orient, its edge is often Eastern.

THE LANGUAGE OF LOVE

Great sex can never take too long, and words can play an important part in beginning and prolonging the love-making experience, whether spoken by characters in a movie or by lovers themselves over a meal, or even during a Medieval bondage ritual.

The language of *The Perfumed Garden* is poetic, evocative; similar conversation skills can open the door to the bedroom. Talk between lovers should be warm, sensual, sometimes provocative. The important thing is that sex is more than intercourse and orgasm is more than rhythmic interplay of penis and vagina. True believers say 'sex' is possible in a crowded room or over a dinner table without even touching.

Foreplay for men was traditionally, in much of the West at least, believed to have been a chore and unsympathetically ignored. This is no longer the case. Foreplay is now known to be as important for men as for women, and there is a bonus for men — a man will have a more intense orgasm if his partner is stimulated to frequent and easy orgasm.

Don't hurry, don't grope — but don't think of the prelude to sex as a solemn occasion. Joke, talk provocatively or suggestively and remember that it is only really by what you say that your partner will know what you do or don't like.

KISSING, TOUCHING AND UNDRESSING

Lip and tongue kissing techniques don't need to be taught — perhaps just perfected. To continue with them through intercourse takes expertise, but is worth perfecting, also.

Chances are both partners will enjoy undressing. Gradually revealing your body is an almost universal turn-on, often even more so if your partner does it for you. Lacy underwear excites men and wearing it stimulates women, who also often like their men to leave items of clothing on, even sometimes, perversely, socks. Stockings, bras,

panties, slips, neckties, camisoles, gloves, scarves, boots, masks are all grist to the fantasy mill and may be more dramatically erotic than the bluest video movie or explicit magazine or book.

Slowly undress your partner — enjoy the perfumes of the garments you are removing; linger and admire each part of your lover's body as it is revealed. Then, if she grabs modestly for an item — a bra say, or he for a corner of a sheet — to attempt a futile cover up, play the game. The rewards will outweigh the delay.

Don't forget, sex can take place fully clothed. Fantasy is for everyone and in foreplay it is probably also worth remembering that some of the most common fantasies for women and men are being involved in group sex, watching others have sex, being watched by others, and watching your partner have sex with another man or woman. In fantasy, the imagination is the only limit.

In reality, heightening sexual excitement usually leads from preliminary kissing and cuddling to intimate fondling and kissing of those erogenous zones: lips, breasts, thighs, buttocks, scrotum, clitoris, penis, anus, ears, toes ... Genital kissing is another art again. Men, almost violently aroused by this torturous petting, find it difficult to believe that for women it is relaxing. But being relaxed is vital in the slower female progression of stimulating and lubricating the vagina for attempted intercourse.

'Kiss, suck, nibble, bite,' said Sheik Nefzawi, beginning an endless list of physical stimulants. Fondle, feel, rub, lick, tickle, blow, wrestle ... Dance naked, or nearly so, for the rhythm of music such as Ravel's *Bolero* is a natural aphrodisiac. And as tongues bathe bodies in passionate embraces, purists in the art of foreplay may care to reflect that the West does not always come second to the East in matters sexual. A kiss — tender, intense, passionate, light — can be, as we know, intensely arousing. It can be the first expression of love.

The kisses which imitate intercourse are celebrated both in *The Perfumed Garden* and the *Kama Sutra*, but much is frowned upon in our modern Western cultures — leading to the sexual fears and inhibitions from which we all suffer to some extent. Some otherwise sexually liberated women, for example, prefer their partners to undress them because the display of their bodies is then passive rather than sexually overt: 'nice girls don't'. Others, reflecting a reaction to traditional female roles, after a lifetime of serving, fantasize about being served by a parade of athletic young men.

Feigning modesty is role-playing. More overt roles can be played before a video or still camera. Couples now pay professionals to photograph them making love. Unless you are madly extroverted, doing it yourself is more relaxed, intimate and probably a better turn-on. The results — your own blue movie or pornographic pictures — can be wildly exciting to look at later. Similarly, amateurs with only the slightest talent can write tantalizing pornographic stories for themselves. Read back at the right moment, they give a whole new meaning to do-it-yourself.

SENSUAL EXPLORATION

Self-exploration is something we are all, or should be, experts at. It is the way we discover our own sexuality, yet many people find it a difficult subject to discuss. Husbands keep their masturbation secret from their wives and vice-versa, as though desiring it or doing it is a signal of inadequacy in a partner. In foreplay, masturbation can be the paramount experience and some devotees say it even beats intercourse. It doesn't, because it is different, but it seems to be accepted that the couple who masturbate each other really well have no trouble with other sexual mores, probably because to do so involves an intimate knowledge of what each partner likes.

Explore with your hands her vagina or anus, or both, stroking gently, entering her with your fingers and even bringing her to orgasm. Stimulate his penis by hand, remembering that men do not have anything like the range of sensation-producing equipment that women have, and attention must be paid to the head of the penis. More women, and some women more often, achieve orgasm through masturbation than through intercourse — that is how important masturbation is. Even if you don't practice mutual masturbation, watch your partner masturbate. Satisfactory sex doesn't only mean intercourse.

EROTIC MASSAGE

Exploring and discovering each other's body through massage is one of the best turn-ons for both men and women, capable of arousing otherwise impotent men and allowing a woman's hormones to build up, preparing her for intercourse. Like masturbation, we should all be experts at massage. For a variety of reasons, often associated with guilt and inhibition, we are not. Like masturbation, too, some couples have been practicing it for ages without realizing what they were doing.

Some would say massage is always sensual. It is not always sexual, however. And not all the most sensual effects come from the most obvious places: fingers, toes, neck, ears, the palms of the hands and soles of the feet can all be stimulated to excitement. Maintain a steady rhythm and constant pressure. Work up from the lower back with flattened hands, alternating the strokes and pressing on the spinal muscles. Lift, squeeze and roll hips, thighs and other fleshy areas. Strike the body lightly with cupped hands, thumbs in and fingers together. With fingers curled into loose fists, knead shoulders, chest, thighs and buttocks, and pummel muscular parts.

He could trace parts of her face with his fingers, stroke her chest and gently cup her breasts in his hands. She could straddle him,

kneading his back with rhythmical strokes, brushing her breasts across his back, running her fingers along his thighs, buttocks, feet.

Creams and perfumes can be brought into play and the massager sliding over his partner's supine form leaves his unique perfume. Massage for sensual arousal should be less vigorous than massage to relax each other (see 'Afterplay'). The problem — if it is a problem —is deciding when massage and the rest of foreplay ends and the 'proper' play begins.

FLIGHTS OF FANTASY

After group sex, the most common sexual fantasy is of bondage — being tied up by your partner for an enhanced orgasm, usually by slow masturbation. Firm but comfortable is the rule for tying. Some are happy to be tied by something as flimsy and sensuous as a silk scarf. Generally, however, something stronger is required to act out the sexual domination symbolism.

Lace stockings are an old favorite, light ropes more practical, and chains and handcuffs probably more part of the fiction than fact. The 'sexual prisoner' is supposed to be able to struggle but not work loose. But it is only a tough and tender game and they must be able to get free in a crisis such as the house catching fire. The scene is then set for all sorts of sexual possibilities and the sensation is said to allow otherwise reticent people to wildly let go (see also 'Loveplay — toys, tools and techniques for imaginative love-makers').

ORAL INTIMACY

Oral sex, like masturbation, is not necessarily all foreplay. It is very intimate, demands a great deal of trust and for many people is the ultimate sexual experience and expression of love. Men are most speedily aroused by fellatio — stimulating the penis by the mouth; women often find the softness of a tongue in cunnilingus preferable to coarse fingers. The sensation, however, can be intense enough to be painful.

Phobias about genital and general cleanliness frequently intrude here. Bathing is the answer but regular partners learn to appreciate each other's odors and tastes and savor the smell of sexual arousal. Sometimes the natural odors are compounded by additions which can be licked up — such as yogurt and honey smeared over the body.

In cunnilingus it is important not to forget to also stimulate your partner's breasts, thighs and buttocks. Often the mouthwork begins here and continues under her arms, between her toes, by sucking her nipples and following a trail to her vagina.

His nipples are similarly sensitive. She can kiss and lick his penis and scrotum. He kisses and explores her vagina, stimulating her clitoris with his tongue and lips. Chances are, at this point, that this is no longer strictly 'foreplay'. Similarly, when she takes the head of his penis in her mouth, sucking rhythmically, ejaculation is a virtually imminent certainty.

Oral sex frequently also includes the anal area. However, with the advent of AIDS, contact with the extremely sexually sensitive anus and its surrounds has become somewhat unfashionable (see 'Safe Sex'.)

BEYOND FOREPLAY

Foreplay, then, is the art on which all that is to follow depends, and even sometimes a conclusion in itself. The Arabian sex expert Kalyana Malla wrote the *Ananga Ranga* at a time when his society was much more rigid than at the time the *Kama Sutra* was written, yet, like his Arabian contemporary Sheik Nefzawi, his motive was similar — to protect couples (in Malla's case, exclusively within marriage) from sexual tedium. Nefzawi unhesitatingly accepts the advice of a woman who confided to 'one of the savants who have occupied themselves with this subject':

> *O you men, one and all, who are soliciting the love of woman and*
> *her affection, and who wish that sentiment in her heart to be*
> *of an enduring nature, toy with her previous to coition; prepare*
> *her for enjoyment, and neglect nothing to attain that end.*
> *Explore her with the greater assiduity, and, entirely occupied with her,*
> *let nothing else engage your thoughts. Do not let the moment*
> *propitious for pleasure pass away; that moment will be when you*
> *see her eyes humid, half open. Then go to work, but, remember, not until*
> *your kisses and toyings have taken effect.*

SCENTS FOR SENSUALITY
AND THE FLAVORS OF PASSION

The use of perfumes, as Sheik Nefzawi wrote in *The Perfumed Garden*, 'by man as well as woman, excites to the act of copulation. The woman, inhaling the perfumes employed by the man, becomes intoxicated; and the use of scents has often proved a strong help to man, and assisted him in getting possession of a woman.'

More than 400 years later, the Sheik's words have a curiously contemporary ring about them as elements of the practice of aromatherapy have spread from the New Agers to even the most conservative households. At the same time, scientists have taken a serious look at the subject of aphrodisiacs, previously only ever treated with skepticism by their profession, and discovered sound chemical reasons for the foods and drinks traditionally accorded the magic powers of inducing love.

The ancients, of course, did not trouble too much about why these scents and flavors had such extraordinary effects — they simply made it their business to know the repertoire and play it to its fullest advantage. The Greeks believed that perfumed plants came from the gods, who were pleased when their fragrances were used. Their custom of crowning Olympic victors with a laurel (or bay leaf) wreath endures to this day. When the Romans emerged, they adopted the Greek enthusiasm for scents such as rose, lily, cardamom, myrtle, marjoram, quince and pomegranate with such a passion that a law was enacted forbidding the private use of such inducements in case there would not be enough left for the deities. Not that this bothered aristocrats such as Cleopatra, who is supposed to have had the floors of her apartment covered with a deep carpet of rose petals and the sails of her barge dunked in rose-water in preparation for her first meeting with Mark Antony. And we need look no further than the Bible to realize the importance placed on the oils of frankincense, sandalwood, cedarwood and myrrh in those times.

♥

On neglecting foreplay

On the matter of foreplay the Sheik was quite contemptuous — and rightly so — of those men who did not go about love-making 'with vigor' and in a way that would ensure his partner's enjoyment.

Such a lover 'lays himself down upon her without previous toying, he does not kiss her, nor twine himself round her; and he does not bite her, nor suck her lips, nor tickle her'.

ESSENTIAL OILS

Rather than going in search of aphrodisiacs direct from nature, modern cupids follow their noses to aromatherapy oil retailers and buy a selection of essential oils. Along with their many other therapeutic benefits, the oils are believed to promote peace and happiness, romantic desire and sexual ecstasy. Oils, by the way, are not exactly oils, when it comes to the essential line-up. They are aromatic substances distilled or extracted from plant materials and, unlike true oil, are as light as water, quick to evaporate and not greasy. Nor are they cheap — the huge volume of petals and the complicated extraction process required to make the queen of oils, rose otto, for example, means that it costs around $10,000 a pint (or 500 ml). Unfortunately, it is a case of getting what you pay for and, according to the purists, the cheaper, chemically synthesized oils simply won't do. Fortunately, a little goes a long way.

The florals — rose otto and absolute, jasmine and ylang ylang — have been used since ancient times for their aphrodisiac powers, as have spicy oils such as cardamom, cinnamon bark, clove bud, black pepper, coriander and ginger. As well, the richly earthy patchouli is said to increase potency and physical stamina, the citrus fruits to engender a general sense of well-being and happiness, and musky angelica incites passion, as do sandalwood and frankincense. The enigmatic, sweet scent of the vanilla bean is the base of many old-fashioned love philters. Whether or not they actually work has been the subject of debate for hundreds of years. But as they certainly don't do any harm, it seems a simple case of enjoying whatever you prefer.

Having assembled an essential oil kit, it is a matter of blending according to your nose — and your partner's, of course. Smell is a powerful memory aid and there is absolutely no point diffusing patchouli all over the house if the object of your desires grew up with it in the 1960s or '70s and can only associate the scent with cramped bed-sits, dirty clothes and long-lost lovers. So let your joint senses of smell arbitrate.

The master perfume makers do, however, provide some guidelines to help you get started. According to these parfumiers who build reputations, not to mention fortunes, by distilling and blending the essences of flowers, herbs and spices, the secret of allure lies in the right balance of notes. An ideal mix should incorporate the top notes of the citrus and floral oils with middle notes from the spice and herb range (plus a few florals such as lavender and violet) with base notes from the woods, heavier florals such as jasmine and animal odors such as musky patchouli.

The experts elaborate further on aphrodisiac qualities by dividing the oils into erogenic, narcotic, anti-erogenic and stimulating categories and decreeing that blends with that elusive power contain elements from each of the four.

EROGENIC AND STIMULATING ESSENTIAL OILS

The erogenics include sandalwood, rose otto and rose absolute, neroli (orange blossom), jasmine, clary sage, oakmoss, patchouli, vetiver and angelica, while coriander, cinnamon bark, ginger, clove, black pepper, elemi and rosemary are regarded as stimulating. (Little wonder, given the line-up from the spice pantry, that many regard a powerful curry as the ideal precursor to great sex — more about that later in this chapter.)

ANTI-EROGENIC ESSENTIAL OILS

The anti-erogenics are those we recognize for their clean, refreshing qualities — lavender, geranium, basil, bergamot, lemon, orange, lime, mandarin, grapefruit, pine, cypress, peppermint, juniper and petitgrain.

On the intimacies
of making love

'When you are close to a woman, and you see her eyes getting dim, and hear her, yearning for coition, heave deep sighs, then let your and her yearning be joined into one, and let your lubricity rise to the highest point; for this will be the moment most favorable to the game of love. The pleasure which the woman then feels will be extreme; as for yourself, you will cherish her all the more, and she will continue her affection for you.'

NARCOTIC ESSENTIAL OILS

Narcotics are sweet and intoxicating. There's some overlap with the erogenic odors in this category, which contains ylang ylang, rose otto and rose absolute, clary sage, chamomile, jasmine, neroli, vanilla, frankincense, cedarwood, sandalwood, vetiver and patchouli.

AROMATHERAPY IN MOTION

Having settled on a suitably appealing blend, the next step is determining how best to use it, and there are countless hours of pleasure to be had in the process. With time, your powers of recall will come into play and favored perfumes will have a multiplied effect of actually stimulating the senses at the same time as reviving previous erotic occasions when the scent was used.

The most obvious place to begin is by applying the potion directly onto the skin (or different potions to different parts of the body). It is best to dilute this potion with some massage oil, as some essential oils can irritate sensitive skin. Next, try using the blend for massage.

To make massage oil, mix your essential oil blend with almond, sunflower, grapeseed or other vegetable oil to the recipe of about 10 drops to just under 1 fl oz (25 ml) of base oil.

A word of warning, concerning massage and motherhood. As many essential oils, including rose otto and rose absolute, cedarwood, angelica and rosemary, are believed to stimulate menstruation, massage using them is perhaps best avoided during early pregnancy when there is a risk of inducing miscarriage. As the oils pass through the skin and enter the bloodstream, many aromatherapists also advise breastfeeding mothers to avoid essential oil massage unless they want to give their infants infused milk.

While flowers may be the traditional accompaniment to ardor, the decided lack of perfume of many hot-house varieties means that following Cleopatra's lead and filling a room with blooms does not necessarily lead to anything other than a pretty sight. While the romance of the gesture of giving flowers will never go astray, one of the more sure-fire ways of bringing the scents of the garden into the bedroom is by essential oil diffusion, either using the electric gadget specifically designed for the purpose, spraying oil-infused water through an atomizer or using heat to release the perfume with a light globe or potpourri simmerer. The latter device, usually an attractive two-tiered ceramic bowl containing a candle with a dish for the oil-infused water on top, has the added advantage of throwing a soft light at night and, if there are decorative holes in the bowl, introducing intriguing light patterns into the bargain. Strew some flowers or petals over the sheets for added visual pleasure and the scene is complete for scaling the sensual heights.

The Perfumed Garden had no doubt about the assets of perfume in enhancing sexual pleasure, describing the erection and decoration of a brocade tent for the specific purpose of seduction:

> *Fill the tent with a variety of different perfumes, amber, musk and all sorts of scents as rose, orange flowers, jonquils, jessamine, hyacinth, carnation and other plants. This done, have then placed there several gold censers filled with green aloes, ambergris, nedde [various perfumes including benzoin and amber, which is burnt over coals]. Then fix the hangings so that nothing of these perfumes can escape out of the tent. Then, when you find the vapor strong enough to impregnate water, sit down on your throne, and send for the prophetess to come and see you in the tent, where she will be alone with you. When you are thus together there, and she inhales the perfumes, she will delight in the same, all her bones will be relaxed in a soft repose and finally she will be swooning. When you see her thus far gone, ask her to grant you her favors; she will not hesitate to accord them.*

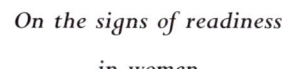

On the signs of readiness in women

'When you observe the lips of a woman to tremble and get red, and her eyes to become languishing, and her sighs to become quicker, know that she is hot for coition; then get between her thighs, so that your member can enter into her vagina. If you follow my advice, you will enjoy a pleasant embrace, which will give you the greatest satisfaction, and leave you with a delicious remembrance.'

25

EAT, DRINK AND BE MERRY

When it comes to the matter of dining before the act of coition, *The Perfumed Garden* is laden with advice, some of it sound, some downright spurious. 'Let your stomach be free from excessive food and drink,' the Sheik decreed, later adding that 'coitus after a full meal may occasion rupture of the intestines'.

While there is no doubting the soundness of his caution for moderation, few would deny the seductive pleasure of anticipating and delaying inevitable sexual congress over a fine meal composed of easy to eat and digest dishes.

Then there are the nuances of eating foods which are sexually suggestive in appearance — women might try peeling and eating a banana in front of their partners, while men might savor figs or juicy fruits such as peaches, melons and mangoes. The sensual delight of

feeding grapes and strawberries or other morsels to your partner might
be your passport to passion, for others, it is the thrill of licking
squashed fruit from his or her body.

The Perfumed Garden is peppered with suggestions for foods to
enhance sexuality, from a three-day fast of egg yolks and onions as 'an
energetic stimulant towards coitus' to boiled asparagus, fried in fat and
poured on yolks of eggs with condiments as a 'stimulant for amorous
desires' and camel's milk with honey taken regularly to cause the
'virile member to be on alert night and day'.

'A man who wishes to copulate during a whole night … may have
recourse to the following recipe,' the esteemed Sheik added. 'He must
get a great number of eggs, so that he may eat to surfeit, and fry them
with fresh fat and butter; when done he immerses them in honey,
working the whole mass together. He must then eat of them as much
as possible with a little bread, and he may be certain that for the
whole night his member will not give him any rest.' Desperate
measures for desperate times. A few chapters earlier, he was
advocating moderation!

References to the sexually enhancing properties of honey and eggs
are frequent throughout history, no doubt for their association with

the reproductive cycles of the animals that produce them. The Roman scholar Pliny declared honey the saliva of the stars and the word honeymoon comes from the old Teutonic custom of drinking honey wine for the first 30 days after marriage, providing, if nothing else, a quick energy boost to fuel the fires of passion. Fruit and nuts, containing as they do the seeds of life, also belong in the lovers' larder and have long been associated with fertility rites. Walnuts, pistachios and almonds all had an important place in the garden of the biblical King Solomon, and were part of a lavish array of foods including honey, aloes, apples and other orchard fruits, wine and grapes which he shared with the visiting Queen of Sheba.

The fruits of the sea have equally important status in the mythology of sensual foods. After all, Aphrodite, the Greek goddess of love, was born of the sea, which could partly account for the long-standing association between eroticism and oysters and caviar.

Since ancient times, the Chinese have placed great store in a combination of diet and herbalism, blending such concoctions as the bald chicken drug, deer horn potion and powdered sea grass with extract of liver of white dog. If nothing else, their protein content was probably beneficial to people whose diet consisted mainly of rice, vegetables and flavorings.

But now the scientists have stepped in with some very plausible, if not a little prosaic, explanations for the foods associated through the centuries with sexual appetite and prowess. So you love chocolate because it makes you feel good? Not surprisingly, the chemists tell us, it contains the so-called happiness chemical, phenylethylamine (PEA). So, incidentally, do some cheeses, salami and rose-water.

A MENU MADE FOR APHRODITE

Our instinctive preference for certain foods is because they mimic pheromones, the chemicals produced by the body to arouse responses in others. Not all of them are sexual, though the ones which concern us here are. They include androstenone, which controls the libido in both sexes and happens to be a chemical relative of the male hormone, testosterone.

Men produce more of this earthy musky scent, but women also exude it, particularly at ovulation time. What does it remind you of? The list reads like an inventory of Aphrodite's kitchen: truffles and other wild mushrooms, game meat, particularly wild boar. Then there are the foods which will leave you smelling of this masculine essence several hours after consumption — asparagus, seeds and leaves of celery, parsnips, not to mention Cabernet Sauvignon and Shiraz (aka Hermitage) or any wine that has been aged in small oak barrels.

Trimethylamine is another potent pheromone, best identified as the smell of decomposing seafood. It is part of the odor of menstruation and turns up in the cuisine of many countries in the guise of blachan and fish sauce of South-East Asia, anchovy sauce in Europe and India's Bombay duck (actually a dried fish). Combined with the excitingly pungent spices of the East — coriander, cumin, chili, black pepper, cinnamon, clove, ginger and nutmeg — it is little wonder that many lovers regard an Asian meal as the precursor to a raging time in bed.

Scientists take the hypothesis one step further, arguing that many foods which men find a turn-on are reminiscent of vaginal odor, while women are subliminally attracted to semen-like smells. So men nominate lime and peaches, bean sprouts, oysters, caviar and seafood generally, and soft-ripened cheeses as their favorite erotic foods, while women list green vegetables such as peas and capsicum, persimmon, yams and mangoes on their menu for arousal. The white wine variety sauvignon blanc also yields this 'freshly mown grass' nose, which possibly accounts for its huge following from the female population.

Champagne is the traditional drink for lovers — and now the experts tell us that it is the sweaty, yeasty notes from the Chardonnay and Pinot Noir grapes that attract us to them. The bubbles provide a touch of frivolity because, after all, sex should be fun. While there is no doubting that a little alcohol releases inhibitions, paramours should heed Shakespeare's warning: 'It provoketh desire, but takes away performance.'

Moderation should also be the keynote when it comes to composing a menu based on the foods of love. The *Kama Sutra* described 'a pleasant meal' consisting of 'a clear soup tasting of mulberries, appetizing grilled meats, drinks of ripe fruit juice, dried meat, lemons and tamarind fruits, according to the customs of the country. Then, at their ease, they drink sweet liquors, while chewing from time to time sweet or tart things.' Depending on the time of day, its modern equivalent might begin with strawberries in Champagne followed by softly scrambled eggs flavored with shaved truffles or salmon roe. Or smoked salmon and asparagus with a lime hollandaise. Maybe a light Japanese snack of sushi or sashimi with wasabi and pickled ginger. For the big fuel-up, try rare roasted beef or game, with truffle jus or a sauce of wild mushrooms, parsnip chips, green peas and a glass of hearty red wine. To conclude? Perhaps an Eastern Mediterranean sweetmeat which combines nuts, honey and rose-water — baklava, Turkish delight and halva spring to mind. Or a light-as-air zabaglione or warm and sensuously frothy eggs flavored with honey. To wash it down? A botrytised dessert wine, luscious with the honeyed taste of ripe fruit. It really is a case of whatever turns you on. How to serve the post-prandial chocolates is another choice best left entirely to the lovers' discretion.

BED BATH TABLE OR TENT

CREATIVE SITUATIONS FOR SEX

If we were to walk into a wealthy person's house in Arabia at the time of Sheik Nefzawi, we might be impressed by the sumptuous drapes and cushions, ornaments and decorations, the number of servants or, for that matter, wives. But what this house would lack noticeably is what we might call 'comfort' and what to us are 'the basics'. Where we live, work and play has changed utterly for most Westerners even in quite recent times. Most people in the East, of course, lived as many still do — in what to us would be abject poverty.

Love-making then was a difficult business. The private room was virtually unknown and there was scant privacy in communal rooms, occupied maybe by several generations of one family or even several families. Sex certainly did not have its present-day recreational role. In Europe, privacy was an 18th-century invention. It has been argued that it was only when the bedroom was established as a realm apart that love became, from an occasional summer activity, an all-year-round pastime.

In the rooms of the past many of the furnishings that are now the tools and toys of today's loveplay did not exist. There were no beds or chairs. Instead, mattresses were laid out at night and put away in the morning. In Japan, instead of sitting on a chair, people rested on their heels in a kneeling position. In Islamic countries they sat cross-legged. Hindus squatted. This made for almost biological differences between them and Europeans who to this day find such positions awkward.

There were no mirrors, tables, wash-stands, cupboards, or pictures on the walls. Often the room was cold, or humid with smoke. The opulence of the establishment would have been signified by the many pretty cushions and beautiful woolen carpets.

LOVE ON A RUG (OR BED) AND OTHER BASICS

On human love-making

'That which is to be looked for

in coition, the crowning point of

it, is the enjoyment, the

embrace, the kisses. This is the

distinction between the coitus of

men and that of animals.'

Love, like much of life in *The Perfumed Garden* setting, took place on the floor (with the baby swinging out of harm's way in a cradle hung from the ceiling). Sheik Nefzawi describes the matter-of-fact procedure: 'If you desire coition, place the woman on the ground, cling closely to her bosom, with her lips close to yours; then clasp her to you, suck her breath, bite her; kiss her breasts, her stomach, her flanks, press her close in your arms, so as to make her faint with pleasure.'

The setting is vitally important for romance. Sex might sometimes be exciting in unlikely and awkward places but, generally, the less comfortable the setting, the sooner you wish it was over. The more comfortable and luxurious, the more you can relax and let love flow endlessly on. Cushions or pillows are still the order of the day: two firmly filled cushions to go pragmatically under the buttocks and two softer pillows for sleeping on, preferably in bed.

Rugs or mattresses on the floor remain a popular traditional setting for sex, partly because the normal modern bed is often too soft, but what would our love-lives be like without beds? Beds make it possible to sleep together. Sleeping together, we can play together, relax together, make love together at any time. So, understandably, beds have become the most common venue for sex. Without them the euphemism to 'sleep around' would be meaningless. But ask a dozen people what their impression of the ideal bed is and you will get a dozen different answers. Soft and silky, say the romantics; hard as you can tolerate, say the sexual avant-garde. High enough to use the sides or low enough not to end up in hospital if you fall out. Bedposts get in the way; bedposts are essential, especially for bondage. There are no hard, or soft, rules and, unfortunately, retailers do not give test drives. You might have to use your instincts to find the bed that suits you, and decorate it accordingly. Remember, the rhythm of waterbeds can be an advantage or a constraint, and electric blankets generally cannot take even modest sexual workloads.

Chairs and even tables were virtually unknown in the Arab world until recent times. Today, ordinary chairs and stools and even bedside tables are brought into use when the seemingly sedate bedroom becomes a sexual gymnasium. Then that fluffy rug on the floor and those strategically placed mirrors on the wall take on a whole new meaning and the bedside cabinet is opened to reveal all the weapons for the battle: lubricants, condoms, corsets, stockings, vibrators, rope, masks. Other than rocking chairs, which have a rhythmical effect not unlike swings, the best chairs for intercourse are well padded and without arms. Swings, of course, are superlative.

BATHROOM BLISS AND OTHER WATERSPORTS

Next in importance to the bedroom in today's Western world is probably the bathroom. In Nefzawi's Islam, as in Caligula's Rome, baths were public and a bathroom was a rare luxury even in European houses until recently. The public baths had well-deserved reputations for the bizarre sexual practices that occurred there, as graffiti on the walls of the baths at Pompeii and Herculaneum show. Often, they go like this: 'Went for a wash, met Flavius, washed him as well.'

Today, in the privacy of our own bathrooms, the practices tend to be sensual, stimulating, caring and creative. The bath is a great venue for foreplay or afterplay — soaping each other, drying each other, giving your partner a bubble bath which focuses attention on the whole body and not only the genitals. But the bath can be seriously restricting for the play itself. Intercourse is possible in a normal bath, but with some danger to life and limb. Watch the plumbing and take care with your elbows. Better still, install an oversized bath or a spa bath, a sauna or Jacuzzi, or fill a tub with hot water and climb in, maybe with friends. And, if it matters, remember that while water does not restrict friction, hot baths reduce fertility by inhibiting sperm production.

If the bath is too tricky, take to the shower where the only restriction on good wet intercourse is a great disparity in height between the players. Even that can be interesting, but hide the slippery soap and don't put any weight on the plumbing. You may care to try it in a pool, a pond or even like seals in the sea where at least the advantage of seeming weightlessness will be more apparent than in a bath.

Cold water may test the woman's power to bring her partner to erection but sex in the surf comes highly recommended. Intercourse is also possible while swimming or scuba diving and underwater kisses have a particularly tangy taste. Even days later, the sand that works its way into your bodily orifices will be a reminder of that sexual romp on the beach.

THE DANGER OF DISCOVERY

Moving outside your own home obviously has disadvantages but, especially if you normally only make love at home in your own bed, can also be wickedly exciting. For some, getting out of bed is a bigger turn-on than getting into it. The office will never seem the same again if you make love on your desk, or in someone else's chair — perhaps your boss's! The danger of discovery is part of the appeal. Some couples are tempted every time they enter an elevator alone.

Other public places tend to carry a high degree of risk, including the risk of assault or arrest, or both. They also usually involve a decision about priority. Which is more important, the sex itself or getting away with the prank? The latter can be addictive, the former does not need it. Public lavatories lack charm. In restaurants there is always the risk of indigestion — yours and the other diners' — and climbing out from under the table is so undignified. Airport lounges offer opportunities but, and for some this is a plus, you never know when you are being watched. As they say, where there's a will there's a way, and in that sense the time and place for love is anytime, everywhere, anywhere.

Aunt Patricia's kitchen sink provides the kind of challenge devotees of sexual escapades relish. Much of the skill, however, is in acting innocent after the event and suppressing guilty giggles every time your eyes meet your accomplice's over the washing up.

Sex of this type, because of its furtive nature, usually comes under the heading of 'quickies'. They need not be furtive but they do, to be satisfactory, need partners who can turn on at much the same rate. Then, when inspiration strikes, make the most of wherever you are.

Women, more than men, seem to find varying the location makes their love-making more stimulating, particularly nights or weekends away from home. It can be holed up in a downtown hotel or on a rug on the hearth of a blazing fire high in a mountain retreat. The important thing seems to be that it is somewhere else. The more romantic the location, of course, the better. So read 'Foreplay with an Eastern Edge' and watch those flying embers.

But when it comes to sex the Western way, the automobile reigns supreme. Some say that's because we get so much training in automobiles during adolescence. They call it 'auto' eroticism. Large autos are almost as comfortable as beds and small ones challenge the imagination as well as human elasticity. Interestingly, while adolescents favor parking lots, mature partners like to be on the move.

Mostly, though, sex might be exciting in forbidden places but for romance, the simple things in life are often preferable. For a chamber of love, nothing beats the bedroom.

LOVE-MAKING POSITIONS
OF *THE PERFUMED GARDEN*

♥

Classic Face-to-Face Positions

THE FIRST POSITION — WITH THE LEGS BENT

This classic face-to-face love-making position offers a slight variation on the so-called, and often much maligned, 'missionary' position, in which the woman lies flat on her back and the man lies on top of her.

In this simple variation, while lying on her back, the woman raises her thighs so that her legs are bent slightly at the knees. Her partner lies between her legs, gripping the bed with his toes for extra support.

This position can be a good one because it easily allows for relaxed, rhythmic strokes. It also lets the man readily adjust the depth of his thrusting so as not to cause his partner any pain. Because of this, it is a position that is extra useful for a man whose penis is long.

Like other face-to-face positions, this is also an extremely intimate one that allows considerable feelings of closeness and hence can be particularly reassuring, especially in the early stages of a sexual relationship. As well, if the man is able to support himself on one arm, his other hand is free to fondle or caress his partner's body or face and provide additional pleasure and stimulation. The woman is able to use both her hands to do likewise for her partner or herself.

THE SECOND POSITION — WITH THE FEET NEAR THE EARS

This variation of the more classic position is particularly useful if a man's penis is on the short side, since it raises, tilts and exposes the woman's vulva, making for a degree of penetration during love-making that gives satisfaction to both partners. It can also provide greater stimulation for the woman, because of the angle at which she is penetrated. As well, the full view of her vulval and clitoral area presenting itself to him may add considerably to the man's excitement.

The woman lies on her back and lifts both of her legs into the air. She then throws them backwards so that each foot is as close as possible to her ears. Because quite deep penetration is possible in this position, make sure the woman is fully aroused before you enter her.

In spite of its advantages, however, this position is not ideal for a woman with lower back problems or a weakness in the pelvic region. It may also be difficult or uncomfortable for some to attain or hold this position, especially if the woman is overweight or pregnant.

THE YAWN

This alternative to the preceding face-to-face position is not included in *The Perfumed Garden* but comes instead from the *Kama Sutra*, another treatise on the art of love-making, though one of ancient Indian

A verse from the Sheik

Although the Sheik often quotes verses from poets, he is moved on occasion to quote one of his own — this on the subject of the kiss.

'The languishing eye

Puts in connection soul with soul,

And the tender kiss

Takes the message from

member to vulva.'

origins rather than Arabian. Its name refers to the way in which the woman's legs are lifted up off the bed and her thighs widely parted.

Rather than lying on top of his partner, however, the man kneels in front of her and, leaning forward, is able to insert his penis into her vagina and begin thrusting movements. The woman can close her legs around his waist, or spread them even wider. You can grip each other's hands if you like, to both support the man in his kneeling position and to offset any instability from the openness of the woman's legs.

Deep penetration is quite difficult in this position and, even though the woman's vulva itself is exposed, her clitoris probably will not receive much stimulation during intercourse itself, so manual or oral caressing may be needed to bring the woman to her orgasm.

THE ELEVENTH POSITION — WITH THE SOLES TOGETHER

Though this position may indeed bring lovers' souls closer, its distinguishing feature is that the woman's feet are pressed together during the course of love-making. It also makes good use of a small cushion, particularly if penetration is difficult to attain when the woman is flat on her back.

Lying down, the woman props the cushion under her buttocks. Then, positioning himself between her thighs, her partner can easily insert his penis into her aroused and slightly raised vagina. Meanwhile, she places the soles of her extended feet together, hooking her legs over those of her lover — which has the effect of opening the vulva even further. This allows not only deep penetration but good stimulation of the clitoris as well. And again, the hands of the woman in particular, since they are not needed for support, can roam and caress freely, either her partner's body or her own.

THE THIRD POSITION — FOR MAXIMUM PENETRATION

This is another variation of the face-to-face, man-on-top lying position in which the woman lies stretched out on the bed or floor and the man kneels between her thighs. She then places one of her legs on his shoulder, and the other over his opposite thigh.

The singular advantage of this position is that very deep penetration is possible. It is advisable, then, that you make sure that you are fully aroused before your partner enters you.

WITH THE LEGS WIDE OPEN

This is a further variation in which the woman thrusts her legs apart. But, unlike 'the yawn' (pictured on page 41), for instance, in this position her clitoris receives much more stimulation from the friction of her partner's thrusting during love-making.

The woman lies on the bed, bends her knees and, lifting her buttocks off the mattress in an arching movement, opens her legs wide. Her partner can then stretch himself above her in a semi-

kneeling position, supporting himself by placing his hands flat on the bed on either side of her.

Because of the depth of penetration that this angle allows, this could be another useful position for the man who feels he might be under-endowed.

It also offers the loving intimacies that other face-to-face positions do — these feelings being heightened, of course, if you do not always close your eyes to each other during love-making itself.

On the importance of the kiss

'The kiss is assumed to be an integral part of coition. The best kiss is the one impressed on humid lips combined with the suction of the lips and tongue, which latter particularly provokes the flow of sweet and fresh saliva. It is for the man to bring this about by slightly and softly nibbling his partner's tongue, when her saliva will flow sweet and exquisite, more pleasant than refined honey, and which will not mix with the saliva of her mouth. This maneuver will give the man a trembling sensation, which will run all through his body, and is more intoxicating than wine drunk to excess.'

Woman Lying on Top

INTERCHANGE IN COITION

So-called because, according to the Sheik, in this position the roles of the woman and the man are exchanged. This classic woman-on-top position requires the woman to take the more 'active' role. It is a good one if her partner wants to be less energetic — as a result of age or tiredness, or simply to vary what has become a bedroom routine.

The man lies on his back, spreading his legs and bending them slightly. His partner then positions herself stretched out and lying between his legs, supporting herself on her arms — as in doing push-ups. She may need to put a pillow under her feet to raise her pelvis a little before guiding her partner's penis into her vagina.

If she then squeezes her thighs together, a tight pressure on the penis will be maintained as she — the more active partner — moves in a thrusting motion, thus bringing her lover to his climax.

Since she has the upper hand, so to speak, in this position, she can alter the direction of the thrusts as it suits her, and in particular can do so in a way that will make sure her clitoris as well as her lover's penis will be stimulated.

Some love-making movements

In The Perfumed Garden six actual movements for making love — as distinct from positions — are described. The effect of any one of them can be intense, both emotionally and erotically, depending on your mood.

The first two are 'the bucket in the well' and 'the mutual shock'. For the bucket in the well, 'the man and woman join in close embrace after the introduction. Then he gives a little push, and withdraws a little; the woman follows him with a push, and also retires. So they continue their alternate movement, keeping proper time. Placing foot against foot, and hand against hand, they keep up the motion of a bucket in a well.'

For the mutual shock, 'after the introduction, they each draw back, but without dislodging the member completely. Then they both push tightly together, and thus go on keeping time.'

See page 73 and page 116 for more of these sexual movements.

WITH THE LEGS ENSNARED

This is a slight variation of the previous position and simply allows the woman, still in the face-to-face position, to once again be the uppermost partner in the love-making.

Rather than the woman lying between her partner's legs, however, the man lies with his outstretched legs 'trapped' between hers.

This posture, like others where both hands are not needed for support, allows for stimulation of the woman's breasts or clitoris and of the man's testicles and nipples — although it is perhaps curious to modern lovers that Sheik Nefzawi never mentions these crucial parts in relation to his love-making positions, no matter how 'advanced' some of them might be.

Similarly, he is somewhat — even if forgivably — remiss in the area of fantasy and sexual play. Nevertheless, these woman-on-top positions offer several possibilities to imaginative lovers. For instance, the woman could partly bind her lover's hands to the bed — though only, needless to say, if he is willing!

WITH THE FEET HOOKED

In this further simple alternative to the preceding two positions, the man can hook his feet over the back of his partner's legs — or otherwise clasp or entwine them together behind her knees — as she lies on top of him.

Doing so keeps the pelvic regions of each partner more tightly pressed together, both heightening the feelings of closeness and intimacy as well as providing more firm support for the rhythmic, perhaps even energetic at times, movements of intercourse.

Woman Astride

THE SCREW OF ARCHIMEDES

The rather ornate name for this position derives — according to notes in the translation of the original text of *The Perfumed Garden* — from an Arabic word which means the pipe or fountain through which water is forced. Like the screw of Archimedes, then, it serves to raise water — or, in the case of love-making, a man's semen — which then issues out of a narrow opening.

To assume this position, the man stretches out flat on his back and the woman sits astride, so that she is facing him. She slides his penis into her vagina and then leans forward, placing her hands on the bed so that she can keep her stomach from touching his. In this supported position she can then move up and down, adjusting the speed and depth of penetration as she wishes.

If she wants to kiss her partner, she simply stretches her arms along the bed behind his head or bends them at the elbows until her lips reach his mouth.

The advantage of this position, as with other woman-astride ones, is that the woman is able to control the thrusting movement which might bring one or both partners to orgasm. In addition, it leaves the man's hands completely free to fondle and caress as he desires.

POUNDING ON THE SPOT

In *The Perfumed Garden* Sheik Nefzawi claims that many people have tried the love-making postures he describes but the most preferred of them all is this one! And although he urges lovers to try a range of different positions in order to establish which ones give their partners the greatest pleasure, he assures his readers that 'pounding on the spot' (pictured overleaf) is the one that the majority of women love.

Essentially it is a sitting position, belly-to-belly, which allows for good penetration and lots of kissing — which well may account for its supposed popularity.

The man sits with his legs stretched out and his partner then positions herself astride his thighs with her legs crossed behind his back. She can then guide his penis into her vagina. As intercourse proceeds she can wrap her arms around his neck while he embraces her around the waist. In this way too, he can help her with the pleasurable up-and-down action as she moves upon his penis. The mutual pleasure can be enhanced even more if the woman contracts her vaginal muscles around his penis with each downward thrust.

WITH THE BACK TURNED

As in the preceding position, in this potentially exciting alternative the man lies on the bed and his partner sits astride him. However, rather than facing towards him, she turns her back on him — quite literally!

From this angle the man can see her buttocks and stroke them or her back. In turn, she can easily fondle his testicles, encircle the base of his penis with her fingers or even stimulate his anal area — if this is a mutually agreeable love-making activity.

THE RACE OF THE MEMBER

There are several sexual positions inspired by horseback riding but in this one it is the woman who mounts the saddle!

The man lies on his back with a cushion supporting him under his head and shoulders, with his buttocks still firmly on the bed or floor. He then bends his legs up so that his knees are near his face, or as

close as he is able to manage. His partner then sits upon him, with her legs on either side of his, lowering herself onto his penis as she does so. She can then, by moving her knees up and down in a horseback-riding fashion, control the pace of the thrusting actions as a rider would the speed of a horse.

RECIPROCAL SIGHT OF THE POSTERIORS

This slightly acrobatic woman-astride position allows — as its name so aptly suggests — each partner a view of the other's buttocks. To achieve this, the man first lies stretched out on his back with his legs

bent and apart. His partner then sits astride him, so that his penis is inside her but her back is turned to his face. The man presses her sides between his legs while she puts her hands on the bed in front of her. Once supported, she can lower her head and look backwards towards her partner's rear, revealing as she does so hers to him.

This is not a very intimate position in terms of being able to kiss, otherwise caress or watch your partner's expressions while making love. But you may find the sight of each other's buttocks adds an extra element not found in other positions. It may also be one which lends itself to sexual fantasy — for either or both of you.

SITTING ON HIS LAP

This is basically a woman-astride, rear-entry position that could easily develop from the delightfully unexpected arousal that sometimes comes with just playing about and being affectionate with each other. It entails both partners being seated.

The man sits on a chair, bench or stool. His partner sits down backwards across his knees, with her legs on either side of his, and facing away from him. She can either slide her vagina onto his penis as she seats herself, or guide it into herself.

This position in itself is not one in which the clitoris is likely to be stimulated as a result of any thrusting. But this should not be too much of a problem since the hands of both partners are left free to stimulate either the woman's clitoris and pubic area or her breasts and nipples. The man can also kiss and nibble the back of his partner's neck or her shoulders, thus providing caresses to further erogenous zones and adding to her arousal.

On the perils of making

love without kissing

'Without kissing, no kind of

position or movement procures

the fullest pleasure; and those

positions in which the kiss is not

practicable are not entirely

satisfactory, considering that the

kiss is one of the most powerful

stimulants to the work of love.'

Rear-Entry Positions

THE SIXTH POSITION — FROM BEHIND

This is a classic rear-entry position, which has several variations. In this version, the woman kneels low on the bed — as if in prayer, according to the Sheik's instructions — supporting herself with her elbows and knees. By parting her legs she presents her vulva to her partner, who kneels behind and enters her.

A disadvantage of this position, as with all other rear-entry ones, is that intimacy of the kind in face-to-face positions clearly is not possible. It does, however — although this is not mentioned in the original text — leave the man's hands free for reaching forward and fondling his partner's breasts and squeezing her nipples.

This may also be a useful position for those women who at times — for instance, during pregnancy — find the angle of face-to-face penetration painful.

On women's indulgence

in passion

'Women are more favored than men

in indulging their passion for

coition. It is in fact their specialty;

and for them it is all pleasure;

while men run many risks in

abandoning themselves without

reserve to the pleasures of love.'

COITUS FROM THE BACK

The Sheik claims 'Coitus from the Back' (pictured on the previous page) to be 'the easiest of all methods' — although he does not say for whom! It is a rear-entry position in which, however, rather than kneeling, both partners are lying down.

To assume it, the woman lies flat on the bed, facing down. She raises her buttocks by propping a cushion under her stomach and hips, thus tilting her vulva slightly backwards and upwards. Her partner can then lie on top of her, being careful to take his weight on his forearms and elbows. During intercourse, the woman can hold firmly onto the man simply by twining her arms around his elbows.

As with the 'missionary' position, this one maximizes the skin contact between partners, and the ensuing feelings of closeness, as the full length of the man's body is stretched out over his lover's.

Note, however, that it is unlikely to be a comfortable position for a woman who is heavily pregnant or whose belly is large.

THE NINTH POSITION — OVER AN ELEVATED SURFACE

Some wisdom on when

to abstain

'Remember that all caresses and all sorts of kisses, as described, are of no account without the introduction of the member. Therefore abstain from them, if you do not want action; they can only fan a fire to no purpose. The passion which is excited resembles in fact a fire which is being lighted; and just as water only can extinguish the latter, so only the emission of sperm can calm the lust and appease the heat.'

This position lends itself to using either high or low furniture in your love-making. As well, it has the additional erotic — and possibly practical — advantage of penetration being able to be easily achieved either almost fully clothed or in a state of semi-undress, thus allowing for those memorable situations where passion simply overtakes you! It has several variations.

For rear entry, the woman leans or lies front down over a bed, table, desk or even the back of a chair or arm of a sofa, keeping either her knees or her feet on the ground, depending on the height of the surface. If she prefers front entry, she simply lies on her back, again with her feet touching the floor or dangling over the edge.

With her legs parted, her partner can then stand between them and penetrate her, grasping her waist and hips for support as he thrusts.

Privacy permitting, you may discover surfaces in the outdoors that are suitable for this position — allowing, on occasion, a spontaneity into your love-making that might otherwise be absent.

MANDARIN DUCKS

This further love-making position from the rear draws on one from the *Tao* — an ancient Chinese text — rather than from the Sheik's more recent treatise. Unlike *The Perfumed Garden*, in the naming of sexual positions the *Tao* draws on the activities or postures of birds, animals and insects. Some of these are quite lyrical and inspirational, and you may want to add them to your love-making repertoire.

This particular side-by-side, rear-entry position clearly gets its name from the mating manner of mandarin ducks. Curled up on her side, knees bent slightly, the woman can be made love to from behind.

Such a position could easily allow cuddling and hugging in bed to develop into something much more erotic. And if a man is enthusiastic about entering his partner from behind but she is not so sure, there is something quite gentle — yet at the same time tantalizing — about this position that might convince her of its pleasures.

COITUS OF THE SHEEP

This position derives its name from an idiosyncrasy of the courtship practices of sheep. In receiving the sexual attentions of the ram, a ewe puts her head down between her forelegs.

To assume this position, the woman is on her hands and knees while her partner, kneeling behind her, lifts her thighs up until her vagina is level with his penis. During actual penetration and inter-

course, the woman then lowers her head between her arms in imitation of the ewe.

Some women may find this position exciting since it adds the extra dimension of visual stimulation. From the position she is in, the woman needs only to look backwards towards her lover in order to witness his thrusts.

LIKE A LATE SPRING DONKEY

Not in the mood for love?

According to Sheik Nefzawi, the following potion — using camphor — is appropriate when you do 'not want to feel the necessity for coition'. 'This substance,' he claims, 'macerated in water, makes the man who drinks it insensible to the pleasures of copulation.' Moreover, continues the Sheik, 'many women use this remedy when in fits of jealousy against rivals, or when they need repose after great excesses.'

This position need not be restricted to any particular season as its name implies — weather permitting! Nonetheless, it is somewhat difficult and, as with other more acrobatic positions, you should take care when attempting it.

Rather than leaning over an item of furniture, in this further variation drawn from the *Tao*, the woman has no means of support in front of her and instead, from an upright standing position, bends well forward with her knees only slightly bent.

This makes for deep penetration, especially if the woman is able to touch the floor with her hands. However, since the man can easily control his thrusting as he stands behind her holding her firmly round the waist, he can make sure that he does not move so hard or so deep as to cause his lover any discomfort or pain.

Not everyone will be able to assume this position, and it may not be to the liking of all either, although the feeling of the man's pelvis pounding against her rear can be sensational for some women. Others, however, even if only partly bent over and grasping behind the knees for support, may not enjoy at all the experience of being made love to in such an up-ended position.

Side-by-Side Positions

THE FIFTH POSITION

This is a classic side-by-side position that is very intimate and can be a delightfully gentle and expressive way in which to make love. Each partner lies on their side, facing each other, but so that the man is

between his partner's thighs. He can then guide his penis into her vagina and witness her pleasure.

In the original text, the Sheik claimed that this position made for rheumatic pains and sciatica, but given that it is one which in fact places very little stress on the body of either partner, it is difficult to see how this might be the case.

Nevertheless, as with any love-making position or movement, if you are in any doubt whatsoever as to its consequences as far as your health or well-being is concerned, it might be best to consult with your doctor or other trained and qualified professional.

Pantaloon dreaming

'Dreaming of pantaloons is ... a sign of protection for the natural parts, and foretells success in business.'

LOVE'S FUSION

This entrancing name could probably be applied with good reason to almost any love-making position. The Sheik, however, used it to refer specifically to a further classic side-by-side position.

In the text of *The Perfumed Garden* it is stipulated that to assume this position the woman should lie on her right side and the man on his left but, needless to say, the choice is entirely up to you. Either way, you each lie on your side, facing each other. Unlike other side-by-side positions, however, in this variation the man's lower leg remains extended on the bed while his upper one is raised over the woman's lower. She then entwines her upper leg around her lover's hip.

Once again, this position allows for the tender making of love, with intimate expressions of affection, which both new lovers and long-standing partners alike adore. It is also a good position for when both partners are tired, or perhaps recovering from an illness or indisposition.

In this slightly different side-by-side position based on one from the *Tao*, you bend your legs around each other, as do fish their tails when spawning. The woman's legs, rather than being flat upon the bed, are raised so that, with her feet close together, they rest across her lover's.

You need to lie side by side at first then, after penetration, the woman, keeping her legs closed, lifts them — with assistance from her partner if need be — so that they partly entwine around his.

In this position, the man can pull his partner's buttocks or thighs towards him, slightly changing the angle of his penis inside her vagina as he does so.

Sometimes side-by-side positions are difficult to maintain for men with shorter penises since they can slip out easily. But there is no harm — and certainly plenty of fun — to be had in making up other versions, thereby inventing sexual positions of your own.

LIKE TWO FISHES

For healthy ejaculation
'There are eight things which give strength to and favor the ejaculation. These are: bodily health, the absence of all care and worry, an unembarrassed mind, natural gaiety of the spirit, good nourishment, wealth, the variety of the faces of women, and the variety of their complexions.'

Sitting Positions

THE FITTER-IN

Rather than one partner astride the other, in this sitting position each partner takes up the same posture. Because of the rocking movement involved, you may find that a firmer surface — like the floor — provides more grip than the softer contours of a mattress.

Both of you sit on your tail-bones (the coccyx, at the base of your spine), with your buttocks barely touching the floor, and facing each other. Then the woman puts her right thigh over her partner's left and he puts his right thigh over her left, or vice-versa.

Each of you then grasps the other round the upper arms and, with the penis already inserted into the vagina, you hold each other and begin a swaying movement, rocking back and forth in unison, in a kind of see-saw action.

Having your feet on a firm surface will help greatly in maintaining both the position itself and its accompanying action, and although your partner's face is at arm's length, there is no reason why you should not adjust your position slightly and lean forward to kiss your partner from time to time if you so desire.

THE ALTERNATE MOVEMENT OF PIERCING

This sitting position with the woman astride and facing her partner is pictured overleaf. Its name refers to the 'come-and-go' movement of the love-making action which is, despite the Sheik's assurances to the contrary, extraordinarily difficult to execute.

To attempt it, the man sits with the soles of his feet pressed together, or he could cross his feet at the ankles. He lowers his thighs and pulls his feet up towards his genital area. The woman then sits down upon his feet, her thighs pressing against his hips and her arms around his neck, while her partner draws her towards and onto him, thus making penetration possible.

The movement in this position is supposedly achieved by the man moving his feet backwards and forwards, or alternatively by pulling his partner back and forth on his penis. Since she is sitting on his feet, trying all the while to take most of her own weight on her feet, this provides the friction, rather than the more usual thrusting movements of intercourse, but do not become disheartened if you cannot achieve this.

Because of the extreme difficulty involved, you might want to experiment with your own variations, perhaps with the woman sitting on a cushion between her partner's feet rather than actually on them.

ASTRIDE A CHAIR

There are many ways to adopt a sitting position when love-making, though it is probably safe to say that the woman really does need to be on top unless her partner's genitals are flexible beyond the realm of most people's experience. From the position of 'the fitter-in' (on page 70), for instance, each of you could lean right back, supporting yourself by grasping each other around the ankles. This enables a mutual rocking back-and-forth movement rather than a thrusting one and so is less orgasm-oriented than many of the positions described by the Sheik, and probably more suited to playing about sexually than anything else.

In a further variation, you could use a chair. The man sits on it and, facing him, the woman sits down upon his knees, sliding his penis into her as she does so. This position opens up all sorts of erotic possibilities, especially since it is an easy one to assume while virtually fully clothed. Hence it has all the makings for impulsive love-making on those occasions when time may be of the essence.

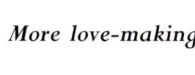

More love-making

movements

Another two movements that could be used during intercourse — as the fancy strikes — are 'the approach' and the rather quaintly named 'love's tailor'.

For the approach, 'the man moves as usual, and then stops.

Then the woman, with the member in her receptacle, begins to move like the man, and then stops. And they continue in this way until the ejaculation comes.'

For the love's tailor, 'the man, with his member being only partly inserted in the vulva, keeps up a sort of quick friction with the part that is in, and then suddenly plunges his whole member in up to its root. This is the movement of the needle in the hands of the tailor.'

Standing Positions

BELLY TO BELLY

This is a classic standing position and, like its variations, can be an exciting one. Many couples discover an additional erotic charge when a position does not necessarily confine them to the bedroom, or indeed to the complete privacy of the home or hotel room. And love-making in a standing position can often mean minimal disrobing is required, and a state of semi-dress — or semi-undress — can be quite arousing. It also allows the possibility for love-making to be more 'of-the-moment' than usual, especially since it lends itself to almost infinite possibilities of location — perhaps even in the scented seclusion of your very own 'perfumed garden' if you are fortunate enough to possess one.

For this position it may help, though it is by no means necessary, if one of you has some means of back support — leaning against a wall or pillar perhaps, or indeed any other secure vertical surface such as a firmly closed door.

Standing upright and facing each other, the woman parts her thighs while the man moves forward towards her so his feet are between hers, one slightly in front of the other. Each partner then grasps the other round the hips or waist, and you can then proceed to make love in this intertwined stance.

For this position the Sheik advises a movement which he calls 'the bucket in the well'. Essentially, this means that the man gives a little push and then withdraws a little. The woman then pushes, and then pulls back slightly. Intercourse continues in this rhythmic, alternating, almost back-and-forth fashion until orgasm is reached or the couple moves on to a further position or sexual act.

On 'the man who deserves favors'

The man who most fits this description is — according to the Sheik's text — 'in the eyes of women, the one who is anxious to please them'. Furthermore, 'he must be of good presence, excel in beauty those around him, be of good shape and well-formed proportions; true and sincere in his speech with women; he must likewise be generous and brave, not vainglorious, and pleasant in conversation. A slave to his promise, he must always keep his word, ever speak the truth, and do what he has said.'

DRIVING THE PEG HOME

The name of this position (pictured overleaf) comes from the action which is like that of driving a nail or peg into a wall. The woman should first steady herself by leaning against a wall or other secure vertical surface. Her partner stands facing her, so that she can encircle his waist with her legs and his neck with her arms. In this suspended position, the man can then enter her.

The couple pictured opposite are not using a wall for support so as to illustrate the position more clearly.

'Driving the Peg Home' would obviously not be a good position for a couple where the woman is much heavier than the man, since he has to both support much of her weight as well as carry out the thrusting movements of coition.

Even so, this can be a thrilling position. It allows for both spontaneity and haste, and has innumerable possibilities for erotic fantasies — to say nothing of their acting out.

IN A SUPPORTED STAND

It is easy to vary the standing position. For instance, rather than being fully suspended, the woman can keep one foot on the ground and simply raise the other, wrapping it around her partner's thigh. Indeed, because this spreads the vulva open, deeper penetration is possible. And if the man holds his partner by the buttocks with one hand and her raised thigh with the other, he can readily control his thrusting movements.

If one partner is taller than the other, simply bend your legs slightly if you are the taller, or stand on your toes if you are the shorter. This may after a while become tiring, however, so it helps if one of you is able to lean against something.

It is also possible to adapt standing positions to a half-stance, in which either partner is supported against a high piece of furniture — the back of a sofa or armchair, for instance, or a chest of drawers or the footboard of a bed.

Don't forget, too, that this position can be a delightful preliminary to further love-making activities, moving from one room to the next, maybe, as the mood takes you.

With Legs in the Air

THE FOURTH POSITION — WITH LEGS ON THE SHOULDERS

This is a further variation of the more classic 'missionary' position — one which allows for the angle of penetration to be easily altered until you find the most pleasurable one for you both.

As pictured opposite, the woman should lie down on her back while her partner kneels between her legs. She then places her legs over his shoulders, thereby raising her entire vulval area off the surface of the bed.

A cushion or pillow can be propped under her buttocks either for additional support, or to lift her vagina even higher.

As with other positions in which the vulva is raised and presented, this one can be an advantage for a man whose penis is small.

WITH LEGS IN THE AIR

This position (pictured overleaf) is not one that allows for much stimulation for the woman, particularly of her clitoral area, but it does have the advantage of providing lots of friction for the man's penis. It is useful, therefore, for those men who need lots of direct, strong stimulation to bring them to orgasm.

The woman should lie on her back and then, with her thighs pressed together, she lifts her legs right up so that the soles of her feet are facing the ceiling and her pubic region is exposed to her partner. He can then crouch before her, his thighs either side of her hips, and in this posture guide his penis into her, all the while helping to support her legs by holding them in the upright position with his hands.

To further stimulate her partner and give him added pleasure, the woman could also try contracting her pelvic muscles, rhythmically squeezing them around his penis — perhaps during quieter interludes between his more vigorous thrustings. As either a prelude to making love or afterwards, the man could reciprocate such pleasure with manual or oral stimulation of his partner's vulva and clitoris.

THE TAIL OF THE OSTRICH

This position (pictured opposite) can be quite erotic — particularly if incorporated into a fantasy — since in essence it involves making love while the woman is as good as upside down. You may, however, need to exercise some caution.

The woman lies on her back along the bed while her partner lifts her legs up until only her head and shoulders are resting on the mattress. He then kneels in front of her and enters her from this position. At the same time she can entwine her feet around his neck and he can grip her buttocks or legs to control his thrusting.

By raising or lowering her buttocks the woman can control some of the penetration and thereby enhance the sensations for either herself or her partner.

Do remember, though, that in this position the woman's back is largely unsupported. This could cause undue strain on her spine or neck and so make sure that you take care, particularly if she has a history of problems in these areas.

With the Knees Bent

THE TENTH POSITION — *ON THE SOFA*

This is one for the living room where you can make full use of a sofa or divan rather than retiring to the bedroom. It also lends itself to a bed with a secure headboard.

The woman sits on the edge of a low seat and reaches behind her to grasp its back with her hands. Her partner stands or kneels before her and lifts her legs to the height of his waist. She then clasps his body by twining her legs around him.

Once securely in this position, the man can enter his partner, taking care not to thrust too energetically since the woman is, after all, virtually suspended in the air with little means of support.

Obviously this is a slightly more acrobatic position than some and, yet again, those with back problems are probably best advised against trying it. Do not forget, though, that there are countless other possibilities for making love in areas of the home other than the bedroom. Many items of furniture readily lend themselves to sexual experimentation and it can be tremendous fun just to discover the possibilities. Safety and good sense notwithstanding, they are limited

WITH THE TOES CRAMPED

only by your imagination.

In this position (pictured overleaf) the woman lies on her back with her legs bent and raised so that both her buttocks and her vulval area are lifted off the bed or floor. Her partner crouches between her legs, gripping — as the name implies — the bed or floor with his toes. As the woman raises her legs, she wraps them round her partner's back and pulls him towards her. For more support, each puts their hands around the other's neck.

Once in this position you can control penetration by pulling away or pushing towards your partner as your love-making proceeds.

On the delights

of the vulva

'Oh how many men's deaths lie

at her door? Amongst them how

many heroes!'

RIDING BAREBACK

In this position (pictured below) the man clings — as a bareback rider would to a horse — to his lover's neck and foot. This is in order to make the thrusting easier from a kneeling position.

The woman lies on the bed with her legs bent and her buttocks slightly raised, while her partner kneels between her legs, his feet tucked up under his rear. After penetration he grasps her in the manner described, one hand reaching forwards and under her neck, the other turned backwards so he can hold her by the ankle.

A refreshing intimacy is possible in this position, allowing you to gaze lovingly into each other's eyes and watch each other's changing expressions as your mutual excitement mounts. Some women also enjoy the restrained — almost 'pinned down' — feeling of being held in this manner by someone they love and trust.

Animal Instincts

AFTER THE FASHION OF THE RAM

Not surprisingly, a number of sexual positions draw on the mating behaviors of animals — for either their inspiration or their name. In this one (pictured opposite), which is essentially a version of the more classic rear-entry position, the woman is on her knees, bending forwards until her forearms are on the bed and her head is quite low down. Her partner then kneels behind her.

During penetration, the woman should press out her vagina by bearing down on her pelvic-floor muscles as much as possible. Meanwhile, the man can support himself by placing both his hands on her shoulders, waist or hips, or alternatively, one hand only, leaving the other free for further intimate caresses of his partner's breasts or perhaps his own testicles in order to heighten the erotic sensations.

This position is a little restrictive for the woman. Since she is using her arms to support much of her weight, her hands cannot reciprocate her partner's stroking. However, if the time for lovemaking has no limits on it, she is bound to get plenty of opportunity to do so.

HE-GOAT FASHION

The name of this sexual posture (pictured overleaf) clearly indicates that the Sheik was perhaps more concerned for the male of the species rather than he was for the nanny.

The woman curls up on her side, then stretches out the leg that is underneath. Her partner kneels between her thighs with his legs bent so that his calves are doubled up under his thighs. He then lifts her upper leg around so that it rests across his lower back. This movement opens the woman's vagina to him from a half-rear position, allowing him to enter her.

For support while he is thrusting the man can hold his partner by the arms or shoulders. She, meanwhile, is in a position where she virtually has little choice but to settle back and simply enjoy being made love to.

LIKE A MARE

This somewhat unusual rear-entry position (pictured opposite) is named after yet another manner of animal coition. It is drawn from the text of the *Kama Sutra* rather than the writings of Sheik Nefzawi.

The man sits on the bed with his legs outstretched and leans back slightly, supporting himself on his hands. The woman sits astride, yet facing away from him, and with her knees bent and resting on the bed beside his thighs.

Obviously the man is not in a good position to thrust, so the love-making actions are entirely up to the woman who, in addition to moving up and down on her lover's penis, could make good use of her pelvic-floor muscles by contracting them, thus encouraging him towards his ejaculation.

This position allows the woman to easily stimulate her own clitoris while her partner can add to her state of arousal by nibbling or kissing her neck and shoulders or by lightly stroking or scratching her back.

Some Acrobatics

FROG FASHION

In spite of its rather odd appearance, this position can be a tender one. The woman should lie on her back, with her legs tucked up under her so that her heels are close to her buttocks. The man sits in front of

her with his legs on either side of hers. Her knees should then be as good as under his armpits.

The man takes his partner in an embrace around her shoulders. As he begins to reach his orgasm, Sheik Nefzawi suggests that the man pull the woman even closer to him, drawing her shoulders gently but firmly upwards to meet his.

At this point you might find it difficult to resist the temptation to lean forward and kiss your frog prince!

On sexual pleasure

It is clear from reading The Perfumed Garden *that, as far as the Sheik was concerned, sexual intercourse was not only deeply pleasurable but moreover a purely natural activity — with no shame or guilt attached. 'Praise be given to God,' he exhorts, 'who has placed man's greatest pleasure in the natural parts of woman, and has destined the natural parts of man to afford the greatest enjoyment to women. He has not endowed the parts of woman with any pleasurable or satisfactory feeling until the same have been penetrated by the instrument of the male; and likewise the sexual organs of man know neither rest nor quietness until they have entered those of the female.'*

THE SEVENTH POSITION — LYING HALF ON THE SIDE

In this further variation of the side-by-side positions, the woman lies half on her side. The man squats between her thighs as she then lifts her upper leg onto his shoulder and keeps her lower one stretched right out between his thighs. This should allow his penis to come into contact with her vagina. By then holding the woman in an embrace with his hands under her back, the couple is able to move together as the man draws his partner closer to his chest.

For some women the half-sideways position may be uncomfortable or difficult to hold. Nevertheless, it is still an intimate posture, allowing you to watch each other's expressions and to respond as you make love to each other.

If there is undue discomfort or pain it is, however, wisest to discontinue and proceed with love-making in either another position or with some altogether different sexual activity.

SPLITTING THE BAMBOO

This love-making position is from the *Kama Sutra*, but since variety is the spice of sexual life — as the Sheik himself only too well knew and advocated — it is included here. As suggested by its name, it relies on the woman alternately raising her legs, one after the other, in a repeated sequence.

At its most basic this is a variation on the preceding position, the woman, however, lying fully on her back. With her partner kneeling in front of her and bending forwards slightly, she first raises one leg and places it on his shoulder, then returns it to the bed and brings up the other to the corresponding position.

She can make this 'splitting' movement as fast or as slow as she likes. No matter what the speed, the action has the effect of gripping the penis and the cumulative sensations can be sufficient to bring the man to orgasm.

Your body needs to be fairly flexible to do this, however, and you may find that your leg muscles tire faster than you might have wished them to. In this event, simply revert to a former position, or try another one. Do not forget that the possibilities are almost limitless.

THE TURNING POSITION

On washing

It is not difficult at times to see that many of our notions about sex may have sprung from The Perfumed Garden *itself.*

Taking the proverbial cold shower, is advice often meted out to those whose lust is perceived to be excessive — or even inappropriate! Thus advises Sheik Nefzawi himself: 'It is bad to wash the sexual parts with cold water directly after copulation; in general, washing with cold water calms down the desire, while warm water strengthens it.'

Rather than being a single position, this is more a sequence of positions — executed to lend variety and perhaps a sense of thrill to a couple's love-making. And, with a bit of patience, perseverance and practice, it is not as difficult as it might at first look.

Start out in the classic 'missionary' position, the man supporting himself on his arms — as he will need to do throughout as the moves progress. He then lifts one leg, followed by the other, over one of his partner's, all the while keeping his penis inside her.

He then begins to turn, still supported on his arms and without withdrawing, until he is lying across her body at right angles. The

On the causes of passion

On this the Sheik was most definitive! 'The causes which tend to develop the passion for coition are six in number: the fire of an ardent love, the superabundance of sperm, the proximity of the loved person whose possession is eagerly desired, the beauty of the face, exciting viands, and contact.'

sensations at this point can be a sheer delight if for no other reason than they might be quite unaccustomed ones.

To complete the sequence, the man turns one more quarter, so that he ends up with his chest between his partner's calves, his head near her feet and his own ankles on either side of her shoulders. Now his partner can easily caress and stroke his thighs, buttocks, perineum, or testicles. She could also try contracting her pelvic muscles, enhancing his stimulation even further.

You can, if you wish, continue turning so that once again you are face to face, from which position you can continue to make love in any of an almost infinite number of ways.

Quite Difficult Positions

THE ARCH OF THE RAINBOW

The somewhat magnificent name of this position rather matches its difficulty. And it looks spectacular if you are able to catch a glimpse or more of yourself and your partner in a suitably placed mirror.

It is not an easy position to achieve, though, since it has an unusual angle of entry and not all couples are able to attain it, since both partners need to be reasonably agile.

On repeating the act

of love

'If you want to repeat the coition, perfume yourself with sweet scents, then close with the woman, and you will arrive at a happy result.'

The Sheik's advice is a touch scanty when it comes to this sometimes crucial matter. If only it were so easy, some men will be heard to sigh! And not without some good cause since it is a well-established fact that on the whole most men find it takes a little longer to get interested again than a woman might. Even so, you may find that the elapse of time and a dose of sweet patience — topped up with some more direct stimulation — will allow you to rise to the occasion once more.

You lie on your sides with the woman's back towards the man. He pushes his penis between her thighs and into her vagina from behind, with his hands resting on her upper back or shoulders for support. The woman then reaches forward and takes hold of the man's feet or ankles, which she gently pulls upwards, drawing him closer to her and making the shape of an arch or rainbow.

Although not altogether intimate, because of the unusual angle, this position may provide new sensations, especially for the woman.

Do not despair, however, if you are unable to achieve this or any other of the more difficult sexual maneuvers. It is worth remembering that the proverbial 'pot of gold' in love-making does not lie in the ability to accomplish the most complicated or acrobatic of positions. Indeed, sometimes the most profound sexual pleasures and satisfactions may be found in the simplest expressions of erotic love.

On menstruation

In spite of its demonstrated grasp of human sexual physiology, The Perfumed Garden is sadly misinformed in regard to menstruation and love-making. Apart from declaring that intercourse during a woman's periods is as detrimental to the woman's health as it is to her partner's, the Sheik upholds that a woman 'feels no pleasure during her courses, and at such a time holds coitus in aversion'. More recent research shows that not only is this not necessarily the case, but in fact that sexual activity — either by self or mutual stimulation — may in fact help alleviate some of the symptoms of menstruation.

THE LOTUS FLOWER

If this looks and feels like you are doing yoga rather than making love then your perceptions would not be far wrong. Deriving its name from that Eastern art, it is a position that not all who try will be able to achieve and those who do, unless very flexible — perhaps after years of yoga itself — may find extremely difficult to hold for very long.

While flat on her back, the woman needs to pull her legs up, crossing them over each other and drawing them towards her body so that her feet are resting on her pubic area. Her lover then kneels in front of her, lowers himself over her and with one leg outstretched behind him enters her vulva.

You could experiment with this position, perhaps trying it with just one of the woman's legs drawn up, or otherwise with a small pillow under her buttocks. If you were in an adventurous mood you could even attempt it with the woman taking up the position near the edge of the bed or a table — taking care of course not to fall off. The man could then stand or kneel in front as he proceeds with penetration.

THE SOMERSAULT

As its name indicates, this is a highly acrobatic position and one in which some sort of variation on it might well be the best option if you want to try it. You could, for instance, attempt it with the woman bending her legs rather than keeping them straight.

In either case, the Sheik, rather oddly to our ears, stipulates that the woman be wearing pantaloons. Although a pair of panties might suffice, most women would probably prefer not to have undergarments over their head during sex.

If wearing them, the woman should drop her panties to the ankles, or to her knees, if you opt for the gentler alternative. She then bends over forwards, so that her head is between her legs, and her neck is caught in the waistband. The man then carefully lifts her and turns her over, in a somersault fashion, gently putting her down so that she is now on her back on the bed or floor. He then tucks his legs under him, kneels in front of her and in this position can penetrate her.

It is possible, or so claims the Sheik, while lying on the back, for some women to place their feet behind their head without the help of either hands or panties! However, not everyone can do this, and in any case it is suggested that you exercise caution. In particular, women with lower back problems are warned against attempting it at all. Certainly, too, the man is ill-advised to seize the woman and as good as flip her over backwards as is implied in the somewhat 'ideologically unsound' language of the translation from the original text!

On the excesses
of love-making

We've probably all been warned at some time in our lives of the general hazards of 'over-doing it'. When it comes to sex though, the Sheik's text offers us some specific words which may not hold up to the rigors of contemporary sexual research although believers in certain 'New Age' doctrines may be more inclined to agree with him.

'Remember that a prudent man will beware of abusing the enjoyment of coition. The sperm is the water of life; if you use it economically you will always be ready for love's pleasures; it is the light of your eye; do not be lavish with it at all times and whenever you have a fancy for enjoyment, for if you are not sparing with it you will expose yourself to many ills. Wise medical men say, "A robust constitution is indispensable for copulation, and he who is endowed with it may give himself up to the pleasure without danger; but it is otherwise with the weakly man; he runs into danger by indulging freely with women."'

♥

On the fulfillment
of conjugal duties

Somewhat surprisingly, given his
informed beliefs on mutual
attraction and the difficulties
that sexual obligation and
making love purely out of duty
entail, Sheik Nefzawi holds in
contempt the kind of woman
who, 'when her husband asks her
to fulfill the conjugal office,
refuses to listen to his demand'.
Similarly, though perhaps more
understandably, he is critical too
of the woman who adorns herself
for the sake of men other than
her lover. 'It is not to please
him,' states the Sheik, 'that she
tries to look well.'

Further Face-to-Face Positions

THE STOPPERAGE

This position is reminiscent of the way a cork stops up the contents
of a bottle, and lends itself to various techniques of foreplay, for
instance, oral or manual stimulation, so long as the woman is able
to remain comfortable holding the position.

The woman lies on her back with a cushion under her buttocks. The man places himself between her legs, pushing his toes against the bed for extra grip. The woman then bends both of her legs up towards her body, as far as she comfortably can, so that her thighs are resting against her chest. The man slides his hands under her arms so as to bring her shoulders up towards him. He can then insert his penis and, as he reaches ejaculation, draw the woman closer to him.

The Sheik suggests that it is perhaps better, however, that this position only be used by those men whose penises are short, or soft, since otherwise it is likely to be painful for the woman. Penetration itself can be difficult and, furthermore, as the penis strikes against the cervix (the neck of the womb) it can cause the woman considerable discomfort. If the woman finds she develops any cramping or pain while attempting or holding this position, it would be wise to desist.

THE SEDUCER

Some might claim that any love-making position worthy of itself deserves this name. Specifically, though, it refers to a further face-to-face one in which the woman lies on her back. But, rather than then simply stretching out upon her, the man sits between her parted legs.

He then lifts and separates his partner's thighs further, placing them as he does so either under his arms or over his shoulders. Once in this position, the man can grasp his partner around the waist or shoulders. This ensures additional support during penetration and its ensuing thrusting.

As with other positions in which the legs are lifted or parted, some care should be taken not to cause any discomfort or pain to your partner. This particularly applies if the woman is pregnant — though pregnancy itself does not mean that love-making need be discontinued.

In fact many women find, often to their great surprise and pleasure, that they become more highly aroused when expecting and hence all the more open to loving and passionate seduction.

THE EIGHTH POSITION — CROSS-LEGGED

In the Sheik's own words, in this position the man mounts his partner 'like a cavalier on horseback'.

The woman lies on her back on the bed or floor with her legs crossed at the ankles and so that her thighs fall apart. Before her partner enters her, the woman bends her legs up and under her thighs. This may, however, prove to be an uncomfortable if not difficult position for some women to assume, let alone hold. In this case you could simply pull your crossed legs back a little, though this would change the depth and angle of penetration as well as the amount of clitoral stimulation you might receive.

Nevertheless, this is a position that offers plenty of scope for imaginative lovers — and it has the additional advantage of leaving the hands of both partners free for further fondling and the intimate caresses of love.

On dreams and their interpretation

Rather oddly, Sheik Nefzawi includes in his text some interpretations of dreams — only some of which pertain to love-making.

To dream of coriander, he says, 'signifies that the vulva is in proper condition'.

On the other hand, to dream of having seen a woman's vulva means, for a man, that 'if he is in trouble God will free him of it; if he is in a perplexity he will soon get out of it; and lastly if he is in poverty he will soon become wealthy.'

103

Erotic Effects

FITTING ON OF THE SOCK

Several of Sheik Nefzawi's descriptions refer to what are more love-making actions than actual positions. In this one (pictured opposite), which for many women results in a state of high arousal, the name derives from the manner in which the penis comes into contact with the vagina and vulva. It is a movement that can contribute immeasurably to the pleasures of foreplay, or perhaps provide a change of pace, or even a separate interlude, during the course of sex. Either way, it can have the effect of arousing a woman deeply before the man fully inserts his penis into her.

The woman needs to lie on her back while her partner squats between her legs with his buttocks resting on his feet. She can then raise her legs and rest her parted thighs across his so that her entire vulval area is exposed and accessible to him.

The man then puts his penis between the lips of his partner's vulva and, using his thumb and forefinger, pulls them closed around it. He then makes shallow but quite rapid thrusts, an action which can be continued until the woman's vagina is moist and fully aroused. Deeper penetration — to the full length of the penis — can then occur. All the while, the man can use his other hand to stimulate his lover's clitoral area. The woman in turn could fondle or gently squeeze his testicles.

THE COITION OF THE BLACKSMITH

The rather curious name for this further love-making movement (pictured overleaf) stems not from how blacksmiths might supposedly go about making love, but instead from the action they use as they withdraw the glowing iron from the furnace and then proceed to plunge it into cold water.

To try it for yourself, the woman will need to lie on her back, not totally flat, but with a cushion placed under her buttocks and her knees raised as far as possible towards her chest. This tilts her vulva towards her partner.

Once his penis is inside her, the man makes the customary thrusting actions of love-making for some time. Then, however, he draws out of his partner's vagina and slides his penis for a moment or so between

her thighs before re-inserting it once more and then, at intervals, repeating the entire movement.

'The Coition of the Blacksmith' (above) and its accompanying action is one that lends itself readily to sexual fantasy and has countless possibilities for the teasing and mutual tantalizing of erotic play.

THE ONE WHO STOPS AT HOME

In this somewhat quaintly named action (pictured opposite) the only real point of physical contact between partners during love-making is that of the genital areas themselves. These should, according to the Sheik, 'stick like glue' to each throughout the course of the coition.

At the outset, the woman lies on her back with her partner stretched out on top of her. His hands should rest on cushions or pillows placed on either side of his lover's shoulders. With the man's penis inside her, the woman raises her buttocks off the bed as high as she can, her partner following this motion with his body. Then she lowers herself to the bed again, but this time in a series of fast, almost jerky movements. All the while, although you are not embracing as such, you should ensure that the penis does not slip out of the vagina by taking to care to move in unison with each other.

Although slightly acrobatic, this position lets the woman set the pace of the love-making. It also gives her a chance to feel that she is the one in control of the movements.

Above all, it is decidedly intimate, depending as it does on close rapport and loving co-operation between partners.

AFTERPLAY

IN THE EASTERN WAY

Remember Sheik Nefzawi's advice from a woman on the importance of foreplay? The same woman, confiding in 'one of the savants who have occupied themselves with this subject' also had advice on the art of afterplay:

After you have got the woman into a proper state of excitement, O men! put your member into her, and, if you then observe the proper movements, she will experience a pleasure which will satisfy all her desires ...
If, by God's favor, you have found this delight, take good care not to withdraw your member, but let it remain there, and imbibe an endless pleasure! Listen to the sighs and heavy breathing of the woman. Then witness the violence of the bliss you have given her.
And after the enjoyment is over, and your amorous struggle has come to an end, be careful not to get up at once, but with-draw your member cautiously. Remain close to the woman, and lie down on the right side of the bed that witnessed your enjoyment. You will find this pleasant, and you will not be like a fellow who mounts the woman after the fashion of a mule, without any regard to refinement, and who, after the emission, hastens to get his member out and to rise. Avoid such manners, for they rob the woman of all her lasting delight.

In other words, don't leap up to walk the dog or watch the ball game on TV. This is for real. This is it. The afterplay is as much a part of the experience as the foreplay.

CONTINUE THE CARESS

It seems ironic that an urge to sleep should be a normal, common response to love-making, but it is, as it is a truism that active lovers don't need sleeping pills. Fatigue follows naturally, particularly in males, from a feeling of being physically and, importantly, mentally drained.

Many women, however, may be mentally supercharged at this time; it is also possible that if the female partner has not reached climax, she will want to experience her orgasm now — or, if she has reached climax, she may want to orgasm again. She may like her partner to masturbate her to orgasm, perhaps by gently stimulating her clitoris, running his fingertips along, under and over it.

As in *The Perfumed Garden*, the *Kama Sutra* also stresses the importance of the signs of affection of the foreplay continuing into the afterplay. So much has changed in the centuries since these treatises were written, but it is humanly reassuring to find so many of the principles have not changed.

Vatsyayana suggests in the *Kama Sutra* that the lovers go separately to the bathroom to relieve themselves and on returning chew betel leaves to scent their mouths while the man rubs an ointment, possibly of sandalwood, into the woman's body. He should embrace her, he says, offer her drink and, conversing warmly, they should take a pleasant meal — a clear soup tasting maybe of mulberries, grilled meats, lemons and tamarinds — and drink sweet liquors. The menu may have changed but a pleasant meal with intimate conversation remains a staple of fore or afterplay today. Even the Book of Proverbs in the Bible has advice on the matter: 'Better is a dinner of herbs where love is, than a stalled ox and hatred therewith.'

As during foreplay, the golden rule for alcohol is to use it sparingly; alcohol is a powerful sedative and Dorothy Parker was revealing her naïveté when she said candy was dandy but liquor quicker. A sip or two of Champagne or a favorite liquor, however, if this is something you enjoy, can be perfect at this time.

MAKE THE MOST OF THE MOOD

What has happened between the foreplay and the afterplay is this: having experienced an enlightening communion, the lovers are off the planet, timelessly cocooned in a satellite of their own ecstasy. Usually there follows a period of intense relaxation and contentment.

But both members of a sexual partnership may not experience the same feelings after sex or, if they do, for the same length of time.

After a deep orgasm, which she savors for what seems like ages, the woman may feel a strong desire to cling to her lover. He, once having ejaculated, may quickly lose his interest in sex and become aware of the world around him; the virile organ, so recently proud and exquisitely sensitive, has become a prosaic and lifeless part of his anatomy and likely to remain so for some time.

This phenomenon is called detumescence (from the Latin, 'to cease swelling'). The blood which flowed into his pelvic area, contracting and tightening his muscles, has now been drained off. The man's detumescence occurs in an alarmingly short time — the penis is flaccid in a minute or so and the lethargy sets in quickly as well.

On the emotional side, there can be a sense of healing, of cleansing, spiritual union or even of being reborn. The more wonderful the experience, the greater the effect. The woman's sexual instinct is said to be so ingrained that she needs to maintain body contact. She wants him between her legs, embracing, caressing, even keeping his penis inside her long after it has lost its former usefulness. Sudden withdrawal can seem to her uncaring, even brutal.

As in foreplay, conversation is crucial to pleasant afterplay. In fact, it is often easier to frankly discuss sexual likes and dislikes, preferred times and places, to describe orgasms and explain fantasies after lovemaking than before. Conversation could be frivolous, romantic, reassuring or just a run of dirty jokes. It is afterplay, after all, and we do not have to be deadly earnest.

A longing to prolong the mood is a natural consequence of intimacy. If music played an important part, play on, sustain the harmony. Back to the basics of books, and magazines and videos, many lovers find that what turned them on in foreplay embellishes the afterplay.

A TIME TO EXPLORE AND EXPERIMENT

Contrary to those who think the thrill of the hunt and one-night climax of the capture is the height of sexual excitement, one of the joys of a long-term relationship is being able to experiment and make new discoveries. Just as a new hairstyle or perfume can be shocking in contrast to the familiar, changes in sexual mores can seem revolutionary, the most simple variation outrageously provocative.

As lovers age they can become less inhibited and even more passionate. There seems always something to look forward to. But even less-passionate sex need not be less satisfactory. The art of the afterplay is likely to be more developed in familiar lovers who know that sex need not always be exciting or, for that matter, that not only exciting sex is good. The earth does not always have to move.

For many women, orgasm is not the ultimate objective of love-making, and older men, especially those who have not kept up regular practice, may not always experience orgasm. However, the delight experienced from giving and receiving physical pleasure is undiminished, never more so than when a couple lie together, confident, complete, after love-making. They savor the afterplay. They know the meaning of tenderness and also frequently appreciate the fun of it all.

Vatsyayana, who in the *Kama Sutra* describes methods of embracing and lying together, speaks of mutual trust born of long association which leads to what he calls sex without barriers. Because of the uninhibited nature of this mutual trust, however, lovers' quarrels can sometimes arise, particularly in the afterplay. To avoid this possibility he suggested the following: don't talk about your other lovers, don't make unflattering remarks about your lover's family and don't use disagreeable words.

WHEN AFTERPLAY BECOMES FOREPLAY

Sometimes, in a sensuous spiral which can take both partners by surprise, afterplay becomes foreplay once more. Conversation alone can do it, as can a sensual post-coital snack. Music, the food of love, may be the catalyst. Kissing, tickling with the lightest possible touch the almost invisible hairs on the skin, blowing, biting, even feigned fighting and wrestling can all do it. Or simply lying quietly in each other's arms, emotionally and physically close and secure. The scent of spent ardor can itself be stimulating.

She may have to masturbate her partner to rouse him, fondling his testicles, sliding a hand up and down his penis, lightly brushing its head with the palm of her hand. The best revivers are said to be skillful manual and oral stimulation with direct suction. Some couples like to complete their love-making by watching each other masturbate, a sort of afterplay by yourself. Being watched and watching at any stage of the proceedings, however, makes it excitingly different from other solo performances.

Massage has been described as making love without intercourse and as a wonderful way of having a safe and loving sensual relationship. It is also one of the best post-coital relaxations. That said, it should be pointed out that it is also often a sure thing to put the afterplay back in the foreplay court. Some say that is the real purpose of afterplay anyway.

The aim of all massage is maximum relaxation. Erotic massage, however, arouses rather than sedates, tending to confirm the belief that maximum feeling in orgasm comes with maximum muscular tension. Relieving massage, while its intentions may be innocent, can easily turn into the rhythmical, ritualised blows of love — massage for sexual arousal. If you are determined that this *is* afterplay and purely for relaxation, avoid the obvious erogenous zones and use more vigorous techniques such as cupping, kneading, stroking, scratching and hacking by brisk chops with the side of the hand on neck and shoulders, back and spine, feet, legs (be careful) and even the head. Better still, take a walk.

IN THE SPIRIT OF THE MOMENT

Understandably, this kind of massage can go on longer than most sensual massages. But if it does go on for an hour or more, the chances are your partner will be too drowsy to return the compliment. If either of you cannot beat the urge to sleep, a final cuddle and a goodnight kiss, at least, might help assuage your partner's emotional needs. Another golden rule in love-making is: don't play if you're feeling down. In afterplay, for example, never give a massage if your partner might pick up feelings of anxiety or anger and reciprocate. There is no place for ill-feeling in love-making and recrimination should never occur. It might not have been the most memorable occasion for her or the fest of his favorite fantasies, but now is not the time to say so. That's not 'play'. Maybe the ideal pastime for afterplay is convivially planning new adventures for next time.

SEX FOR ALL SHAPES AND SIZES

In spite of the good number and variety of positions described in the original text of *The Perfumed Garden*, Sheik Nefzawi readily admits that some of them 'cannot well be put to the proof'. Nevertheless, he says, even if you cannot manage them all — for whatever reason — there are still plenty to choose from. He also suggests invention and experimentation for anyone who thinks his list is 'not exhaustive'. Whether you might exhaust yourself in the process, though, is another matter altogether.

In a rather curious note, too, he adds that he has not included any positions that he thinks are impossible to assume, and cites the more convoluted positions from the *Kama Sutra* as examples of such as these.

Even so, in some ways, the 16th-century Sheik was well ahead of his time. Most of his positions can at least be attempted by anyone in reasonably good health, and whose body height, weight and shape is not too different from that of their lover's.

This may not necessarily be the case, however, when it comes to lovers whose bodies may be quite different from each other. In a section appended to his descriptions of 'possible' love-making positions, Sheik Nefzawi outlines some further variations for those whose bodies are 'of different conformation'.

Contrary to the impressions given to us by the media, as well as the beauty and fashion industries, no two bodies are the same — and there is no such thing as the perfect one, either. Put any one person with another, and suddenly it becomes clear that the range of body types and sizes is enormous, and the combinations almost infinite. In other words, although the Sheik intended these following variations for those whose bodies were of some extreme type, if you and your partner are having difficulty with any position, you may want to include some of his suggestions in your love-making practice.

115

THIN MAN, LARGE WOMAN

Further love-making

movements

The final two movements
included in The Perfumed
Garden *are the curiously named*
'the toothpick in the vulva' and
'the boxing up of love'.

For the toothpick in the vulva,
'the man introduces his member
between the walls of the vulva, and
then drives it up and down, and
right and left. Only a man with a
very vigorous member can execute
this movement.'

For the boxing up of love, 'the man
introduces his member entirely into
the vagina, so closely that his hairs
are completely mixed up with the
woman's. In that position he must
now move forcibly, without
withdrawing his tool in the least.'
The Sheik — having saved perhaps
the best till last as so many of us
are wont to do — comments that
this is the movement that women
prefer 'to any other kind, as it
procures them the extreme pleasure',
adding that it 'appeases their lust
most completely'.

The Sheik offers four suggested positions for 'the coition of a lean man and a corpulent woman'. These, incidentally, could be equally useful when the rotundity of pregnancy begins to make its presence felt.

SIDE BY SIDE AND FACE TO FACE

In order to make love to his partner in a sideways face-to-face lying position, the man could, once they are lying next to each other, lift her uppermost thigh as high as possible and rest it over his hip. Her lowermost arm becomes a pillow for his head, supporting it slightly off the bed. Then he props a firm cushion or pillow under his lower hip, thus raising his pelvis — and his penis — to the height of her vagina.

WOMAN LYING AND MAN KNEELING

If the woman's belly is so large that it falls down over her thighs and sides, the Sheik suggests the woman lie flat on her back instead. She can then bend her legs up towards her stomach, so that her partner can kneel between them. Holding her around the waist, he then pulls her towards him. If he still is unable to penetrate her vagina, he could slide his arms under her buttocks, lifting her up slightly in this fashion.

This is not a totally successful position, however, as the Sheik himself grants. Mainly this is because the woman cannot really move. And, as well, the woman should take care that her thighs do not wrap around her partner otherwise, if they are very heavy, their weight could prevent him from making thrusting movements.

WOMAN ON HER SIDE

Another sideways position is offered. The woman lies on her side, her lower leg slightly in front of the other. Her partner then crouches down onto that leg so that his penis is in line with her vagina. By raising her upper leg and bending it slightly, her vagina will open sufficiently to allow penetration. Holding her legs in this position, the man can then slide his penis into her as he lies between her legs.

REAR-ENTRY SIDE POSITION

The Sheik specifically recommends this alternative during pregnancy. The woman needs to lie on her side, her legs together. She then bends them up slightly towards her stomach. It should then be quite easy for her partner to penetrate her from behind, though he may need to raise his leg to the height of her thigh, particularly if her thighs are large.

LARGE MAN, THIN WOMAN

'In the case of the man being obese, with a very pronounced rotundity of the stomach, and the woman being thin, the best course to follow,' advises the Sheik, 'is to let the woman take the active part.' To this end he offers two positions, though it is worth keeping in mind that any of the woman-sitting-astride positions could prove useful.

WOMAN ON TOP

The man lies on his back with his legs together. His partner then lowers herself onto him, sliding her vagina over his penis. She can

Windows and shoes

Dreams of windows and shoes,
according to the Sheik's
interpretations, are both to do
with women. If a man dreams of
climbing through a window or
putting on a shoe, he most
certainly will soon have a young
woman or a virgin for his lover,
if, in his dream, the window has
been recently installed or the
shoe is new. But if the window
has been there a while or the
shoe is well-worn, then he is
more likely to end up in bed
with an older, more
experienced woman!

then proceed to move in any action that brings them both pleasure. The Sheik advises that the woman rest her hands on the bed but she could use her fingers to stimulate herself or her partner further.

MAN ON TOP

If you want to try the man-on-top position, the woman needs to part her legs slightly and the man should kneel between them, with his legs bent up and tucked under him, his buttocks resting on his feet. It is not the easiest maneuver and, what is more, you might also find that the man tires easily and that full penetration is quite difficult.

Similarly, in a side-by-side position, it may not be possible to achieve deep penetration.

LARGE MAN, LARGE WOMAN

When it comes to both partners being 'corpulent' and wanting to make love, 'they cannot contrive to do it without trouble,' claims the Sheik, 'particularly when both have prominent stomachs.' Nevertheless, the always-imaginative Sheik illustrates yet again his rather sound grasp of both anatomy and bodily function and recommends two positions.

REAR ENTRY, WOMAN AND MAN KNEELING

The best way to try, he says, is for the woman to be in the kneeling position, with her rear raised. Her partner should then be able to enter her from behind, resting his belly, if needs be, on her buttocks. Even so, he might need to place a cushion under her knees — or even his own — in order to achieve the right height for penetration.

REAR ENTRY, SIDE BY SIDE

The woman could lie on her side and be made love to from behind. She must, however, be able to draw her legs up enough so that her vulva is exposed and at an angle whereby penetration is possible.

Wisely, the Sheik suggests that even if both partners are on the large side but not overly so — or perhaps if they each imagine they are — there is no reason why they should not attempt any position they care to. They could, however, he warns, find that they get weary easily and become breathless, and therefore a delayed orgasm, after much thrusting, will leave them feeling quite fatigued.

VARIATIONS IN THE HEIGHT OF SEXUAL PARTNERS

Having dealt with discrepancies in bodily weight, *The Perfumed Garden* goes on to offer helpful advice 'for when the heights of lovers are at odds with each other'. The Sheik once more admits that such positions can prove quite exhausting for each partner. He also points out that one of the drawbacks faced by lovers of different height is that of being unable to comfortably kiss — be it in either a standing or any other love-making position.

Three positions are offered as being ones where a tall man and a short woman, or a short man and a tall woman, can continue kissing while making love.

An anecdote on inspiring

affection

The Perfumed Garden

contains many anecdotes and

short exemplary tales — related

by the Sheik usually to make

some particular point about the

art of making love.

One such — on inspiring

affection in a woman — is this:

'It is reported that a man,

having asked a woman what

means were the most likely to

create affection in the female

heart, with respect to the

pleasures of coition, received

the following answer:

"O you who question me, those

things which develop the taste

for coition are the toyings and

touches which precede it, and

then the close embrace at the

moment of ejaculation! Believe

me, the kisses, nibblings, suction

of the lips, the close embrace,

the visits of the mouth to the

nipples of the bosom, and the

sipping of fresh saliva, these

are the things to render

affection lasting."'

MAN ON TOP

The woman needs to lie on her back, placing a thick cushion under her buttocks and another under her head. She then bends her legs up as far as possible towards her chest. With her partner lying on top of her, he can then insert his penis, grasping her by the shoulders as he does so and pulling her towards him. To help hold this position, the woman should entwine her arms and legs around his back.

SIDE BY SIDE, FACE TO FACE

For this alternative, both partners need to lie on their sides, facing each other. The woman can then slide her lower leg under her partner's side, pulling it upwards as she does so. The other thigh she places over her partner's, pushing her stomach out in an arching movement while he guides his penis into her. For support, each of you should hold the other around the neck. As well, the woman can cross her legs around the man's back, pulling him close to her as she does so.

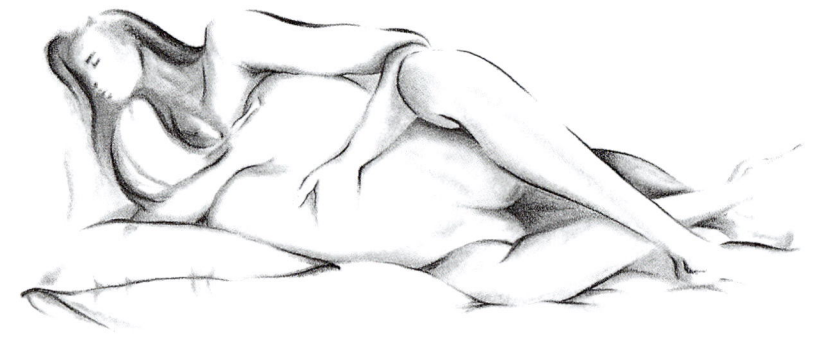

WOMAN ASTRIDE

In this further suggested position, the man lies on his back, with his legs stretched out. His partner sits astride him, then, once she has guided his penis inside her, lies down on top of him, while raising her knees to the height of his stomach. Supporting herself by placing her hands on his shoulders, she can then push up the rest of her body.

You are likely, even so, to run out of steam quickly in these positions. Bearing this in mind, remember that, with some experimentation as far as love-making positions go, you and your partner are bound to find ones which allow for the differences in your bodies and yet which still give you the profound mutual pleasures of a shared experience — including the freedom to kiss and caress as you choose. It is simply a matter of trying them out — including all those other ways to show your sexual love for each other that do not involve penetrative intercourse.

OTHER PHYSICAL DIFFERENCES

It is worth noting, too, that Sheik Nefzawi outlines some possibilities for lovers who have various kinds of congenital conditions, mostly of the back and neck. He also devotes some brief space to those who suffer from paralysis — and astutely suggests that if only the lower limbs are affected and the spinal column is still sound, then all manner of positions could be safely tried, except those where the afflicted partner would need to stand. This might mean that most of the movements of love-making are up to the other partner, but in a loving relationship this could hardly be considered a problem.

If you are in any doubt, consult with your doctor, refer to other, more detailed informative material on the subject, or speak with a trained specialist sexuality counselor. Talk to your partner, too, of course, feeling free to express your desires as well as any doubts you may have, working together to overcome any real or imagined 'hiccups' in your love-making.

Above all, perhaps, keep in mind the noteworthy remark from *The Perfumed Garden* itself:

> *Sometimes most enjoyable coition takes place between lovers, who, not quite perfect in their proportions, find their own means for their mutual gratification.*

Wise words indeed from one who clearly had some inkling of what he was talking about.

Sex and Pregnancy

Of all the gratuitous pieces of advice doled out to first-time parents, the most annoying is the one that goes something like: 'Make the most of your time before the birth, as your life will never be the same again.' Even more infuriating is the realization five days, five months, even five years after the baby is born, that the pundits were right.

BEFORE

A baby can bring almost miraculous joy that is impossible to imagine in pre-parenthood days. But the transition from couple to family involves an adjustment of equally unimaginable proportions, and one not many people survive without a few glitches along the way. Sure, you can still go to work, out to dinner, travel, play sport and enjoy a good sex-life with a baby in tow. But it takes a bit more planning. Nowhere does this have greater impact than in the bedroom.

Most of the advice concerning pregnancy in *The Perfumed Garden* concentrates on confirming the pregnancy and determining the sex of the fetus. 'If there is any doubt about the pregnancy,' the Sheik counseled, 'let the woman drink, on going to bed, honey-water, and if then she has a feeling of heaviness in the abdomen, it is a proof that she is with child. If the right side feels heavier than the left one, it will be a boy. If the breasts are swelling with milk, this is similarly a sign that the child she is bearing will be of the male sex.'

Other signs that 'it's a boy' were 'if the woman remains in good health from the time her pregnancy is certain, if she preserves the good looks of her face and a clear complexion, if she does not become freckled … the red color of the nipples, the strong development of the breasts, bleeding from the nose, if it comes from the right nostril'.

Indicators of a girl included 'frequent indisposition during pregnancy, pale complexion, spots and freckles, pains in the matrix, nightmares, blackness of the nipples and a heavy feeling on the left side'.

DURING

While the modern medical profession would probably take issue with all of the above advice, any couple who has experienced difficulty conceiving will identify with the anxious search for 'signs' — of ovulation, conception and healthy pregnancy. Some couples whose lives have been ruled by thermometers, calendars and trips to the gynecologist report that their sex-lives drastically improve when conception has occurred and spontaneity is once more an acceptable bedfellow.

Others feel overprotective of the fetus they have worked so hard to create, and fear (in most cases entirely erroneously) that intercourse will in some way harm the baby.

On the other hand, many couples for whom pregnancy has previously been something to avoid, find sex without contraceptives a liberating experience. For others, the notion of the woman's fecundity is a turn-on, further enhanced by the excitement of having made a baby. This creates a new sense of intimacy and more enjoyable sex.

If the woman is suffering from morning sickness, however, it is doubtful there will be much sex at all. It would be hard to imagine a greater turn-off than the woman having to interrupt the proceedings for a quick vomit as another wave of nausea strikes. Coupled with tiredness, sore and expanding breasts, a changing body shape and increased vaginal lubrication, the first trimester of a pregnancy can be a trying time for parents-to-be, and one when the man's understanding and sympathy can be tested to its limit.

Fortunately, though, morning sickness is not confined to the mornings, it rarely lasts all day and symptoms do not often persist beyond 12 weeks. It is a time to start practicing the flexibility which will be all-important after the baby arrives and finding the right time to make love is an even greater challenge. If you feel like death warmed up at night, try in the morning or vice-versa, and make the most of the hours when you feel vaguely human during the weekends.

As a general rule, sex during pregnancy is not just okay, it is downright beneficial. The baby is well protected in a sealed bag of waters and at most it will feel a gentle rocking during orgasm. As it experiences the same contractions much more intensely during labor, which can last for up to 24 hours, without any harm, the dangers of routine sex are next to nonexistent. As long as you both feel up to it, sex keeps you and your partner close, fit, and prepares the woman's pelvic muscles for delivery. It is best, however, to take extra care during oral sex not to blow air into the vagina, as this can cause an embolism or air bubble which could be fatal to both mother and baby. Nor should a woman have sex with someone who has a sexually transmitted disease (STD) which could be transmitted to the fetus.

There could be occasions when your doctor or midwife will advise sexual abstinence. This may be the case if you have a history of miscarriage or premature labor. Oxytocin, the pituitary hormone released by women during sexual arousal also causes uterine contractions and, in some cases, may stimulate labor. There is also some evidence that the prostaglandins in semen may start contractions if the cervix is ripe. This is by no means a sure-fire way of inducing labor (as many couples who have tested the theory when their babies are overdue will testify).

Other occasions when sex will be off-limits include if the woman is experiencing any bleeding or pain, if the cervix is dilated or the membranes have ruptured and amniotic fluid is leaking, in the later stages of a multiple pregnancy or if the condition placenta previa is detected (when the placenta is in an abnormal position over the cervix and could be dislodged by intercourse).

If you are warned off sex, make sure it is clear whether the doctor means for the short or long term and if he or she is advising against penetration or orgasm or both. If everything is forbidden, the woman can still enjoy intimacy with her partner by masturbating him or performing oral sex. Or the couple might try intercourse between the thighs.

RECOMMENDED POSITIONS

There comes a stage in practically every pregnancy when it is no longer possible to ignore the bulging belly. Positions that make it easier include rear entry with the woman on all fours, or lying side by side like nesting spoons, or the various woman-on-top options.

Sheik Nefzawi favored rear entry: 'When the woman's belly is enlarged by reason of her being with child, the man lets her lie down on one side; then placing one of her thighs over the other, he raises them both towards the stomach, without their touching the latter; he then lies down behind her on the same side, and can thus fit his member in. In this way he can thrust his tool in entirely, particularly by raising his foot, which is under the woman's leg, to the height of her thigh.' More considerate of the woman's comfort is for the man to sit on a chair with his lover astride and facing him. This way she can control the depth of penetration so long as her feet touch the ground. Another possibility is for the woman to sit or lie with her buttocks on the edge of the bed and feet propped on a chair. The man then stands between her legs facing her. Some couples decide that getting round the mountain is just too hard in the last couple of months of the pregnancy. Instead, they opt for mutual masturbation or simply lots of cuddles and lying close together to sustain them until after the birth.

AFTER

At the risk of stating the obvious, giving birth is a monumentally physical experience. With everything and everyone focused on getting the baby out, there are probably few occasions when a woman is more engrossed in what is going on with her body. Midwives often comment on the sight of the enlarged exposed clitoris during labor and some women find that the breathing pattern they establish with the rhythm of their contractions is very similar to that of sexual arousal and the approach to orgasm. But while giving birth is an intensely gratifying experience, getting over it and adjusting to life with a baby is another matter altogether.

Before delivery, the question uppermost in most couples' minds is: 'How soon after the birth can we resume sex?' In the immediate weeks after the birth, the question is more likely to be: 'Does it ever resume?'

The answer is: 'Yes, as soon as you both feel you can manage it.' Medically speaking, as soon as the cervix has closed and the vagina healed of any tearing or episiotomy, or in the case of a cesarean delivery, the incision has mended, it is fine to return to your pre-pregnant sex-life. Some doctors add that it is wise to abstain until bleeding from the site where the placenta was attached to the wall of the uterus has stopped. This happens around the same time, between two weeks and two months after the delivery. However, many people say that the real time it takes to get back a normal sex-drive is more like two years.

Loss of libido is, however, very common and there are physical and psychological reasons for it. While vaginal tears or scars may have healed well, the site remains tender long after the stitches have come out, and the prospect of penile penetration can alarm some women. The best approach is to take things very gently — the woman could insert her own or her partner's finger very gently into the vagina to relax the muscles before introducing the penis. This fear can escalate to vaginismus (involuntary contraction of the muscles) which makes penetration impossible, so if time doesn't heal, seek expert advice.

On the nature of women

'Woman is like a fruit, which
will not yield its sweetness until
you rub it between your hands.
Look at the basil plant; if you
do not rub it warm with your
fingers it will not emit any
scent. Do you not know that the
amber, unless it be handled and
warmed, keeps hidden within its
pores the aroma contained in it.
It is the same with woman. If
you do not animate her with
your toying, intermixed with
kissing, nibbling and touching,
you will not obtain from her
what you are wishing; you will
feel no enjoyment when you
share her couch, and you will
waken in her heart neither
inclination nor affection, nor
love for you; all her qualities
will remain hidden.'

Other physical problems which can arise following birth are sore and cracked nipples from the rigors of breastfeeding and hemorrhoids from straining during delivery, neither of which is likely to make the woman feel very sexy. Then there is the lowered estrogen level from breastfeeding, which can leave the vagina feeling dry and irritated — a problem that can usually be solved by using a water-soluble lubricant.

It can also be a bit of a shock to discover that oxytocin (the hormone released during arousal which also causes uterine contractions) is also responsible for the let-down of breast milk. This can range from a mild leakage to a spurting geyser and can either be a turn-on or a complete turn-off. Wearing a maternity bra to bed is not likely to make a woman feel like a sex siren, so maybe this is the time to indulge in a bit of flirtatious modesty and invest in some sensuously slinky lingerie that feels good and flatters the figure.

The good news about breastfeeding (and sexual arousal) is that oxytocin also helps the uterus contract to its normal size, which is the first step in regaining your old body shape. A gentle exercise program is a good idea and the sooner it starts, the better for both mind and body.

Men, too, have problems adjusting to the responsibilities of fatherhood and also to their partners as mothers. Many say that having witnessed the traumas of the delivery, they find it extremely difficult to regard the vagina as an organ of pleasure rather than the birth canal.

There are many other adjustments to be made before you will feel entirely comfortable in the new life as parents who also have a fulfilling sex-life. There is the feeling of loss of control which many a woman will experience, particularly if she is adjusting to being financially dependent for the first time in her adult life, and a majority of women suffer some form of postnatal depression, though most recover to find a new life of greater fulfillment. If you do not think this is happening, you should seek counseling immediately.

The prime reason, however, for failure to enjoy or even get around to sex after the birth of a child, is because many new parents are simply too exhausted to contemplate it. Giving birth is the hardest physical work a woman will probably ever do in her life and hospitals are not the best places to get the type of rest a new mother needs. Nor, for that matter, is home, where the parents are busy adjusting to the constant demands of a baby, interrupted sleep, well-intentioned visitors, endless nappy washing, and possibly returning to work at the same time. Little wonder that this is the time when an already stressed relationship is most likely to collapse. It is also a time when both partners have to learn to make sacrifices and focus on maintaining intimacy and conversation in what little time they have for each other.

Babies seem to have an in-built radar which tells them when their parents are even thinking of sex, so it is often better to actually hire a baby-sitter, or ask a relative or trusted friend to take the infant for an afternoon so you can indulge yourselves in the luxury of coitus without the interruptus. The benefits for the parents of some time to themselves are passed on to the baby in the form of happier, more relaxed people when they are all back together again.

If the woman starts to feel sex is just another task she has to perform, it is likely she will try to avoid it. When it is a case of simply trying to reserve what little space is left for themselves, a couple might find masturbation is the short-term solution for their sexual needs. If, however, the woman recoils every time her partner comes near her, the man will feel rejected and the relationship will suffer. It could mean both are missing out on a lot of relaxing touching and hugging which leads to better sleep when you can get it and a greater capacity to deal with the baby when you need it most.

Fortunately, the news on postnatal sex is not all negative. Some women find that in the period immediately following birth the congestion due to increased blood flow to the pelvic area creates a feeling of sexual readiness. The downside of this heightened responsiveness is that it can leave a residual feeling of fullness even after orgasm. In the longer term, women often say that the desensitizing experience of pregnancy, delivery and postnatal checks leads to a general loss of inhibition which translates to better fun in bed. Particularly as you have probably discovered new positions and turn-ons during pregnancy, the overall result can often be increased sexual adventurousness.

On the frequency
of love-making

It should occasion no surprise that
The Perfumed Garden has
something to say on the question of
just how often one should have sex
— a question no doubt wondered,
if not asked, many times over in
this world. His response though is
far from the more evasive, or even
exaggerated, ones we might be
familiar with.

Men of 'phlegmatic or sanguine'
temperament should not make love
more than two or three times a
month; while those of a 'bilious or
hypochondriac' nature only once or
twice a month. Nevertheless it is a
well established fact, says the Sheik,
'that nowadays men of any of these
four temperaments are insatiable as
to coition, and give themselves
up to it day and night, taking
no heed how they expose themselves
to numerous ills, both internal
and external.'

What might he make of research
that indicates a wide range of
frequencies of love-making?
Certainly, how often you have
intercourse, is only up to you and
your partner to decide.

127

SAFE SEX

Rather than it being an exclusively modern trend, there is evidence that the symptoms and consequences of 'copulation sickness' have been acknowledged since early Egyptian times. And although we are more familiar with the terms venereal infection or sexually transmitted disease (STD), 'copulation sickness' was the term used at the time Sheik Nefzawi was penning *The Perfumed Garden*.

On the subject of sexual health, the Sheik confined his advice to the matters of *aiguillettes* (impotence), 'vigor for coition' and treatment for 'sterility in women'. For the former, Sheik Nefzawi recommended potions ranging from 'nutmeg and incense (oliban) mixed with honey', or 'pyrether, nettleseed, a little splurge of cevadille, ginger, cinnamon of Mecca and cardamom taken in honey' and a beverage made by macerating chickpeas in a liquid of onion juice and honey which was guaranteed to render 'his member rigid and upright without intermission'. For the latter, remedies included rubbing the woman's sexual parts with a piece of linen which had the marrow of the hump of a camel spread on it. This treatment concluded with the woman drinking the juice of the 'fruit of the jackal's grapes' (or black nightshade) mixed with a little vinegar while fasting for seven days.

In this less superstitious modern decade, however, we have the concept of 'safe sex' — any form of sex that avoids the exchange of bodily fluids. Since many of the methods for avoiding contact with your partner's semen, vaginal secretions or blood are not 100 per cent safe, the more accurate term is 'safer sex' — meaning an approach to sex that minimizes the risks by carrying out the protective measures as responsibly as possible.

THE CONCEPT OF 'SAFER' SEX

Safer sex involves using protective barriers — condoms or latex shields (dental dams) — for all forms of penetrative intercourse and oral sex. As infections can be transmitted through small cuts or scratches on the hands or fingers, it is also advisable to wear latex gloves if you plan inserting your hands or fingers into the vagina or anus during loveplay. It also means doing this every time you have sex, as one contact is

enough to infect or become infected with an STD. And while the gay community has been hardest hit by the arrival of AIDS, the heterosexual world is very much at risk. Even monogamous couples have to revise their attitudes, as statistics indicate that more than half of the people in so-called monogamous relationships experience outside affairs. And as most of these are on the sly and never admitted to, it requires mutual total trust to continue having unprotected sex, even with your life-long partner. It is, in the end, a decision that can only be made as a couple.

Some of the choices can be made easier, however, by categorizing sex acts according to the risk involved. In the no-risk section belong all the non-penetrative aspects of love-making — cuddling, massage, masturbation and telephone sex. Then there's simulated intercourse, in which most couples can climax by rubbing bodies together, placing the penis between the thighs or breasts or using toys (your own, not shared) such as vibrators or dildos to bring each other to orgasm. Bathing together, and kissing and stimulating each other's genitals by hand (so long as you are wearing latex gloves) are also safe.

Vaginal intercourse using a condom and a spermicide containing nonoxynol–9 belongs in the low-risk category. Ejaculating outside the body is an added precaution against breakages. Anal licking or kissing and cunnilingus using dental dams are similarly only mildly risky, as are sexual activities involving urination, tongue kissing if either of you has mouth ulcers or sores, and fellatio using a condom. It should be noted here that pre-seminal fluid has been found to contain HIV, albeit in a lower concentration than semen, but it still renders coitus interruptus (orally, anally or vaginally) unsafe.

Anal intercourse, with or without a condom, is a high-risk activity. So are vaginal intercourse without a condom and spermicide, unprotected fellatio, cunnilingus and sucking the breasts of a lactating woman. Sharing penetrative sex toys is also not worth the risk, nor is inserting your hands or fingers into your partner's anus or vagina a good idea if you aren't prepared to wear latex gloves. Love bites, or any sexual play that draws blood, such as scratching, is also not on.

STDs — SEXUALLY TRANSMISSIBLE DISEASES

Most sexually transmissible diseases (STDs) other than AIDS present more of an inconvenience than a threat to life, though some are indeed potentially fatal if not treated. All STDs require medical attention.

AIDS stands out in this category as the only STD for which there is no cure and, for this reason, is dealt with in much greater detail later in the chapter.

CHLAMYDIA

This is an infection that affects both men and women. You can have it without having any symptoms — so you can also unknowingly pass it on. In men, it usually presents as an inflammation of the urethra, which makes urination painful. Both sexes may notice a discharge. In women, if the infection spreads from the cervix to the uterus and Fallopian tubes, it causes pelvic inflammatory disease (PID) and considerable pelvic pain, and can affect fertility. Treatment is a course of antibiotics.

GONORRHEA

Another disease that can be symptomless, gonorrhea can also be unintentionally transmitted to sexual partners. Men, however, usually notice burning on passing urine and then a discharge from the penis. Women may also have vaginal discharge or lower abdominal pain. The cure is a course of penicillin, unless the strain is penicillin resistant, in which case other drugs are available.

SYPHILIS

This disease advances in three stages. The first is heralded by a sore on the genital region — on the penis, vagina or in the rectum. Even if the sore disappears, unless it has been treated, the disease remains. If untreated, some weeks or months later the sufferer will notice a skin rash, hair loss, a sore throat, or lumps around the lymphatic nodes (in the thighs, armpits and neck). Diagnosis is confirmed with a blood test and treatment is a course of penicillin. If it is still untreated, or lapses into a dormant phase, syphilis will progress to its tertiary stage which affects the nervous system, heart and blood vessels leading to the heart, and can ultimately cause death.

CYSTITIS

Cystitis is an infection of the bladder that can occur when coliforms (bacteria) from the bowel are transferred to the bladder during sex. It used to be known as the honeymoon disease, because many women experienced the complaint in the burst of unaccustomed sexual activity following their wedding day. Symptoms are a frequent urge to pass urine and burning during urination. Treatment is a course of antibiotics. Drinking lots of water and urinating after intercourse can also prevent the disease, by flushing out the bacteria before they take hold.

THRUSH

Also known as candida or monilia, thrush is a common fungal infection that afflicts mainly women, though in men it presents as red spots or a rash on the penis. Women experience vaginal itching, a white, curd-like discharge from the vagina and sometimes burning during urination.

On arousal

'Before setting to work with your wife excite her with toying, so that the copulation will finish to your mutual satisfaction. Thus it will be well to play with her before you introduce your verge and accomplish the cohabitation. You will excite her by kissing her cheeks, sucking her lips and nibbling at her breasts. You will lavish kisses on her navel and thighs, and titillate the lower parts. Bite at her arms, and neglect no part of her body; cling close to her bosom, and show her your love and submission. Interlace your legs with hers, and press her in your arms.'

On 'premature' ejaculation

The question of what is actually meant by 'premature' ejaculation aside, the Sheik had this to say of the man who reaches orgasm shortly after penetration:

'He gets upon her before she has begun to long for pleasure, and then he introduces with infinite trouble a member soft and nerveless. Scarcely has he commenced when he is already done for; he makes one or two movements, and then sinks upon the woman's breast to spend his sperm; and that is the most he can do. This done he withdraws his affair, and makes all haste to get down again from her. Such a man — as was said by a writer — is quick in ejaculation and slow as to erection; after the trembling, which follows the ejaculation of his seed, his chest is heavy and his sides ache.'

Treatment is anti-fungal creams applied locally or vaginal pessaries. Intercourse should be avoided during treatment, particularly if you are relying on barrier protection using rubber or latex for contraception.

GARDNERELLA

Antibiotics are used to treat gardnerella, a vaginal infection which is usually detected because of an unpleasant-smelling discharge.

CRABS

Not the aquatic variety, these crabs are lice that infect the pubic hair and cause intense itching. Unless treated with creams and medicated shampoos, they can spread to other parts of the body and bed partners.

HERPES

Herpes is the virus which causes cold sores around the mouth. Genital herpes is caught when the virus is transferred by direct contact between the genitals and another's cold-sore-affected mouth or genitals. The symptoms start with an itchy, painful tingling sensation which develops into blisters before becoming small open sores. Once you have been infected the virus remains in the body, often breaking out when the sufferer becomes ill or stressed. There is no cure, but there are creams to relieve the symptoms, and the attacks usually becomes less severe after a couple of years. Zinc cream can help stave off an outbreak if you recognize the symptoms early enough. The sores usually heal in about 10 days. Until then, sexual contact should be avoided.

Genital herpes is most threatening during pregnancy as the baby can become infected during its passage through the birth canal. This can lead to brain inflammation (encephalitis), which could leave the baby mentally and physically impaired. For this reason, any woman who suffers from genital herpes must be closely monitored during the last month of pregnancy, and if an outbreak occurs or appears imminent, the baby will be delivered by cesarean section.

GENITAL WARTS

Genital warts are rarely a problem if they remain small. Big ones, however, can make intercourse difficult and painful. They grow on the penis, vulva and around the anus and are spread through unprotected contact during intercourse. Treatment by a doctor involves painting them with a plant extract, or burning or freezing them off.

AIDS

There is as yet no cure for AIDS, the condition that can develop from HIV infection. The virus attacks the body's immune system, and renders it unable to fight off infections. As a result, common infections become much more threatening. Current evidence suggests that 35 per cent of people infected with HIV will develop AIDS within seven years. Within the same period, a further 35 per cent will develop symptoms associated with HIV, but not fulfilling a diagnosis of AIDS. For those who remain without symptoms it is uncertain whether they will continue to do so.

Up to three weeks after infection with HIV somewhere between 50 and 90 per cent of people experience an acute viral illness which manifests with bad flu or glandular fever-type symptoms. Others do not experience any symptoms. Although it is difficult to generalize about symptoms of the next stage of the disease (because many of them are indicative of a host of other illnesses), they include significant, unexplained weight loss (at least 10 per cent of body weight), swollen lymph glands in two or more places not including the groin and which persist for more than three months, unexplained fever, chills, drenching night sweats and persistent diarrhea.

AIDS is diagnosed when the immune system is so badly affected that the person develops opportunistic infections or conditions rarely found in people with fully functioning immune systems. Most common are a form of pneumonia called *Pneumocystis carinii* pneumonia (PCP) and a skin cancer called Kaposi's sarcoma. Even at this advanced stage, the infections are not necessarily terminal, as the arsenal of drugs to combat them is growing daily. Although the virus is incurable, antiviral drugs and lifestyle changes are believed to prolong the life of a person with HIV. For this reason, anybody who suspects they have been in contact with the disease is encouraged to have a blood test, which is called the antibody test.

If the test is positive, it means you are infected with the virus which, medical miracles aside, will remain in your system for life. You can infect others by bringing them in contact with your bodily fluids (that is, semen, vaginal secretions or blood). If the result is negative, it means HIV antibodies were not detected in your blood because you don't have the virus, or you have been infected so recently that you have not yet made antibodies. (Usually a person starts making the antibodies from two weeks to two months after being infected.)

Many couples choose to have the antibody test before they begin their sexual relationship. Cautious couples also elect to continue protected or safer sex practices, even when they receive a negative test and intend the relationship to remain monogamous. Medical opinion varies on whether HIV or antibody-positive people should have unprotected sex with other antibody-positive people, as the virus can mutate and there is a risk of picking up a more damaging strain, or another STD which could hasten the progress of the disease.

The most common ways of transmitting HIV are through unprotected sexual intercourse, sharing needles or syringes, during pregnancy and birth or via breast milk. It is not spread through the air, by mosquitoes or through normal social contact with HIV-positive people. You cannot, as far as anyone knows, get HIV from toilet seats, swimming pools, sharing bed linen or towels, holding or shaking hands, hugging, cheek kissing, or even tongue kissing (unless you have scratches or open cuts inside your mouth), sneezing, sharing a glass or cutlery, or giving or receiving blood (in any country where you are sure proper sterilization procedures are observed). It would, however, be unwise to share razors or toothbrushes with an HIV-positive person, because of the risk of free blood being present on the utensils. Also, exercise commonsense care when it comes to cleaning up blood spills.

Intravenous drug users should always use a new syringe or, at worst, one which has been cleaned using the 2 x 2 x 2 method (flush twice with water, twice with household bleach and twice with water). The greatest risk of transmitting the disease comes when one intravenous drug user passes the needle on to another user for immediate reuse.

Estimates of the length of time the virus lives outside the body range from several seconds to several minutes, so the chances of catching HIV by, say, standing on an infected syringe at the beach are extremely remote. You are more likely to end up with tetanus. There is a slight risk of HIV being transmitted through needles used for tattooing or body or ear piercing, which can be avoided by proper sterilization procedures. Likewise, any sex aids or bedroom toys should not be shared and should be thoroughly cleaned between uses — diluted household bleach, soap and hot water and hydrogen peroxide will do the job satisfactorily. Be sure to rinse with water after cleaning.

Babies of mothers with HIV are born with HIV antibodies and it takes two years to know whether they are positive — the length of time before uninfected babies lose their mothers' antibodies. An estimated 20 to 50 per cent will be infected during pregnancy and there is further risk that they can become infected if an HIV-positive mother breastfeeds.

USING CONDOMS AND OTHER PROTECTIVE MEASURES

The most effective ammunition in the battle against AIDS and all other STDs is information — closely followed by latex. That means condoms, latex barriers or dental dams and gloves. To be extra safe, use them in conjunction with a spermicide that contains nonoxynol–9 (N–9), which is known to destroy a wide variety of STDs. Some condoms are actually lubricated with the chemical, which is not toxic, and while it does not taste brilliant, it won't hurt you if you ingest it during oral sex. If you need to use extra lubricant, make sure it is a water-based or water-soluble product such as KY Jelly, Muko, Lubafax or Wet Stuff. Oil-based products such as massage oils, petroleum jelly (including Vaseline), baby oil and Crisco will cause latex to weaken and possibly tear, defeating their purpose.

Like all unfamiliar acts, using condoms and other protective latex products takes a bit of getting used to, but with practice, putting it in place can become an integral part of foreplay. And it is best to deal with it before the interlude becomes too heated and you are in such a hurry that you don't do it properly.

Many couples actually grow to like condoms, as men find the slightly reduced sensitivity actually delays ejaculation while the ring at the base of the penis helps maintain the erection. Fellatio is often less inhibited as condoms remove the squeamishness many people suffer about swallowing ejaculate. There are colored and flavored condoms to make the process even more enjoyable. Models with ribs and nobbly bits for 'increased stimulation' should be avoided, however, as they might not fit properly and may allow semen to leak out during intercourse.

APPLYING A CONDOM

To put a condom on, begin by gently massaging the penis to erection. Open the packet and remove the condom. (Always check beforehand that they are within their use-by date and that there are no obvious signs of deterioration.) Squeeze out any air from the tip of the condom by pressing it between the thumb and forefinger — a bubble can cause the condom to split. Then place the condom over the head of the penis with one hand and roll it down the shaft with the other. If uncircumcized, push back the foreskin first.

After climax, the penis should be removed from the vagina or anus before the erection has subsided, and the wearer should hold the condom rim firmly in place against the base of the penis as he withdraws so as to avoid any leakages. The used condom should then be wrapped in a tissue and disposed of in the trash — if it is flushed down the toilet, chances are it will clog the system.

OTHER LATEX PRODUCTS

The protocol for latex shields or dental dams used during oral sex is similar, though many users wash the sheets of latex, which are about 5 inches (13 cm) square, first, to remove the unsavory rubbery taste. The shield should be spread over the entire anal area or vulva and it must not be reused. Plastic food wrap is not an adequate substitute as it punctures easily and can slide around as the action develops.

LOVEPLAY

TOYS TOOLS AND TECHNIQUES FOR IMAGINATIVE LOVE-MAKERS

Aphrodisiacs may have been prized by the ancients, but sex aids as we known them today were unimaginable. *The Perfumed Garden* has few references to equipment beyond pillows and when it does talk about accessories, they usually play a part in sexual contortions which would defy an Olympic gymnast. Not even Sheik Nefzawi insists that these positions are possible, claiming instead:

It is said ... there are women of great experience who, lying with a man, elevate one of their feet vertically in the air, and upon that foot a lamp is set full of oil, and with the wick burning. While the man is ramming them, they keep the lamp steady and burning, and the oil is not spilled. Their coition is in no way impeded by this exhibition, but it must require great previous practice on the part of both.

While we find it difficult to imagine sex aids without batteries, latex or silicone, previous civilizations were not entirely bereft of sexual hardware. In China, both penis rings (made of carved jade or ivory) and tinkling balls (worn in bunches under the skin of the penis) appear in erotic literature from the Ming Dynasty (1368–1644). The job of penis rings, fitted around the base of the penis, was and still is to maintain erection and delay ejaculation. In the absence of today's elastic materials, they had to be secured by a strip of fabric slipped between the legs and tied around the waist. Modern versions include ticklers for added clitoral and labial stimulation.

Maintaining erection is also the role of the sheath, wrapped or strapped around the shaft of the penis, some versions of which function as penis extensions. A more specific, even intimidating, piece of equipment is the penis enlarger — a vacuum pump fitted over the penis for a brief period each day which is said to both lengthen and thicken the member. The San Francisco Pump is probably the best-

known model. Used for 10 minutes per day, the change is said to be perceptible after six months.

Delaying ejaculation is also the purpose of mildly anesthetic desensitizing sprays which are applied directly onto the penis. Many men find the slightly reduced sensitivity when wearing condoms has a similar effect. Condoms and spermicides, however, have become essential ingredients of any safe penetrative sex and the technology is constantly improving. Colored and flavored condoms remind us that safe sex can also be fun. Beware, though, that ribbed, contoured and rippled models are not recommended for either safe sex or contraceptive purposes, mainly because of their irregular fit and the possibility of leaks.

In the East, at the time of *The Perfumed Garden,* tinkling Chinese balls, also known as exertion bells, Burmese bells or *rin-no-tama* in Japanese, were inserted under the skin of the penis after it had been cut. Their principal use was as an enlarger, although women were also known to insert them vaginally before sex. The aristocracy had elaborately gilded silver ones while the poor made do with toxic lead.

Such balls became popular with Western women in the 18th century. Today's versions, normally two or three plastic or sometimes metal balls joined by a string for easy removal, are inserted into the vagina for intense stimulation capable of lasting, if you can stand it, all day. Thai beads — made up of a string of 15 to 20 smaller beads — are a variation of this theme.

The subtly erotic novels of the Ming Dynasty bear little relationship to the explicit books, magazines and videos available for sexual stimulation today. These are particularly useful for rekindling the sometimes jaded appetites of long-term relationships. Reading aloud to each other continues a tradition that goes back to the ancient teachers. Some say watching a suggestive movie with well-played and directed erotic scenes can be infinitely more exciting than poor-quality straight porn. For a variation, partners might try making their own videos or stills.

Alongside the erotic literature and films, vibrators, dongs and dildos occupy a major section in any sex-aid store. They come in an ever-increasing variety of shapes, sizes, colors and textures, some with electric motors, some with several different movements and dual controls and, in the case of dildos, some cast from famous real-life models! Vibrators are not exclusively a sex-aid and are widely used in all sorts of massage. In fact, it is not necessary to use a phallic-shaped vibrator for sexual stimulation; many find less specific versions equally sensuous.

Most couples using vibrators, however, prefer the shaft shape, as do women using them as masturbatory tools. Women can use them externally to stimulate the clitoris or other parts of the body or internally to simulate intercourse. In rear-entry heterosexual intercourse women sometimes use vibrators to provide the clitoral stimulation which may be lacking. Both men and women can use them anally. Size, shape and type is really a personal preference but first-time users are usually ad-

vised to begin with a basic model and not to be overly ambitious. In standard models the battery and motor are usually contained within the shaft. The more advanced multi-function vibrators, sometimes programmed by computer chips, usually have two motors and are operated by a separate control panel. They vibrate, rotate or swivel — some even light up — and many have a two-pronged design which means they can be inserted simultaneously in the vagina and anus. Others may be used by two people at the same time. Slip-on attachments are available and, like irons and hairdryers, there are scaled-down travel models. Vibrators, with their stimulating movement on the clitoris and vagina, can excite women, and men, before intercourse and assist women who have difficulty reaching climax or are seeking further orgasms.

Dongs and dildos are penis substitutes, some with scrota, strapped on or used manually. Traditionally made from rubber or latex which can be realistically molded and painted, recent models are often made from harder-wearing, non-absorbent silicone. Because silicone can be boiled, it has hygienic advantages. The advent of the leather harness has made wearing dildos more comfortable than its predecessor which relied on a G-string made from elastic bra-type straps. The harness fits over the pelvis with a hole in the front to hold the dildo and is secured by straps around the waist and thighs. Lubricants can be useful here. Most today are water-soluble and many come in a range of flavors.

The Venus Butterfly is another strap-on aid. Shaped like a butterfly, it sits against the clitoris and vulva stimulating the wearer for as long as she wants to keep it on. Because the same device comes in different shapes it is sometimes called a stingray or a dolphin.

Butt plugs are used primarily in male homosexual activity but some heterosexual couples find them useful for anal sex. Usually made of latex, they are inserted into the rectum to enlarge it or to maintain its size in readiness for penetration. Butt plugs, sometimes called screws, come penis-shaped, diamond-shaped, pink with glitter or in numerous other guises and some have motors that make them vibrate.

Male blow-up dolls usually have separate vibrators because the fabric of the doll will not inflate adequately to create a firm penis. Female dolls are far more common and are usually used as masturbatory aids. They can, however, turn an adventurous twosome into a makeshift threesome and some people find that working out fantasies on a doll releases inhibitions. Others are excited by seeing their partner with a doll. Artificial vaginas called merkins, unlike dildos, tend to be mechanical rather than true replicas. They are usually shaped from plastic or rubber and include a container for warm water.

Clothes have an important psychological impact on love-making. Worn provocatively, they are an exciting part of the fantasy and,

removed erotically, a practical part of the ritual. And the look and feel of fabrics — the gloss and texture of taut black leather, the soft sensuality of fur — can also become a powerful turn-on. While slinky, silken fabrics next to the skin are considered a sensual stimulant for men and women today, Sheik Nefzawi counseled against 'silken cloths worn by women' which could 'affect injuriously the capacity for erection of the virile member' — the mind boggles.

Although we tend nowadays to make love, at least ultimately, naked, our sexual wardrobe would nonetheless astound him. Any item can be provocative in the right situation but among those designed for the purpose are leather and rubber garments stretched revealingly over the breasts, pelvis and backside. Buckles, chains and studs add an element of toughness or suggest domination or threat. Long boots and high-heeled shoes play a similar role. Wet garments also emphasize the body's shape, as does much erotic underwear.

G-strings ideally should cover the entire pubic region but nothing else. The best women's models undo from the sides with hooks or ribbons and the best men's with Velcro fastenings. In both cases, they are designed for high-speed and easy removal. Crotchless knickers, of course, side-step the problem by not having to be taken off in the heat of battle. Corsets and bustiers, while they have lost some of their attraction (mainly because they were plain uncomfortable — women, too, need to be able to breath during sex), also emphasize the female form. Strangely, given their disadvantages, some men like to be laced into them.

Stockings have been an almost universal turn-on seemingly forever. Usually black and worn with a lacy suspender belt, the desire to take them off is overwhelming. Much the same applies to uniforms — be they school, nursing, police or military — and to the chastity belt, now making a reappearance in some circles after centuries in the dungeon. It should be remembered that the chastity belt was originally more a measure against rape than a protection of property. These days the challenge is to achieve climax without removing it.

Food can also be a powerful weapon in the love-making arsenal and you might like to turn yourself into a human strawberry shortcake, covering the parts of the body you would like to have licked and sucked with whipped cream and decorating it with strawberries.

If you prefer more explicit imagery, shops selling sex toys usually have a range of 'naughty candy', from the all-day-sucker-style Dick on Stick to anatomically shaped chocolates such as Cream-centered Willies and Boobs. Or you might try messing about with some ice cubes. Some people find the sensation of ice running all over the body exquisitely erotic, but for others it could be just plain torture, so proceed with caution. And never, ever, use dry ice, which might smoke seductively but also sticks to the skin and burns like the devil.

Following the thin line between pain and pleasure, it is interesting to note that being tied up, albeit with consent, is one of the most common fantasies. Adult toy shops purvey a sophisticated range of equipment, including hoods, gags, clamps for the nipples and genitals, racks and beds with stocks to secure the wrists and ankles. For most lovers, however, a few silk scarves, bathrobe cords or strips of sheeting are ample for even their most fervent bondage fantasies. Beware of materials that cut or burn and knots that won't undo in an emergency. If you are serious about bondage it is probably worth investing in a tailor-made belt with quick-release buckles. And remember, never leave anyone tied up for more than about half an hour and, certainly, never on their own or face-down.

While for most people having the pace and timing of the climax dictated by another is turn-on enough, discipline in the form of beating and whipping is a common adjunct. Specialty shops stock paddles and whips which make plenty of noise without doing too much damage. However, never forget that it is a game.

INDEX

Main reference given in bold.

Italics show pages on which photographs appear.